Overcoming Grief and Loss After Brain Injury

Overcoming Grief and Loss After Brain Injury

Janet P. Niemeier, PhD, ABPP • Robert L. Karol, PhD, ABPP

OXFORD
UNIVERSITY PRESS

2011

OXFORD
UNIVERSITY PRESS

Oxford University Press, Inc., publishes works that further
Oxford University's objective of excellence
in research, scholarship, and education.

Oxford   New York
Auckland   Cape Town   Dar es Salaam   Hong Kong   Karachi
Kuala Lumpur   Madrid   Melbourne   Mexico City   Nairobi
New Delhi   Shanghai   Taipei   Toronto

With offices in
Argentina   Austria   Brazil   Chile   Czech Republic   France   Greece
Guatemala   Hungary   Italy   Japan   Poland   Portugal   Singapore
South Korea   Switzerland   Thailand   Turkey   Ukraine   Vietnam

Copyright © 2011 by Oxford University Press, Inc.

Published by Oxford University Press, Inc.
198 Madison Avenue, New York, New York 10016

www.oup.com

Oxford is a registered trademark of Oxford University Press

Library of Congress Cataloging-in-Publication Data

Niemeier, Janet P., 1947–
    Overcoming grief and loss after brain injury / Janet P. Niemeier, Robert L. Karol.
        p.; cm.
    Includes bibliographical references and index.
        ISBN 978-0-19-538895-4   1. Brain damage—Patients—Rehabilitation.
    2. Brain damage—Psychological aspects.   3. Grief.   4. Loss (Psychology)
    I. Karol, Robert L.   II. Title.
        [DNLM: 1. Brain Injuries—rehabilitation.   2. Brain Injuries—psychology.
    3. Psychotherapy—methods.   4. Stress, Psychological—rehabilitation. WL 354 N6720 2011]
        RC387.5.N54 2011
        617.4'81044—dc22

                                                                        2010014500
    ISBN-13: 9780195388954

9   8   7   6   5   4   3   2   1
Printed in the United States of America
on acid-free paper

Preface

Grief is a common human experience. It is not unusual or abnormal. Yet, despite being so common, it is often misunderstood. This is never more evident than when grieving loss after brain injury. You survived; you are alive. But it is hard to explain your injury and your support system may be lost. Moreover, if you have sought help in coping with grief, the health care providers you encounter may be perplexed as to how to help. Should you appear depressed or anxious, there are known protocols and treatment pathways, both through psychotherapy and medication. Not so with grief after brain injury.

We wrote this book after having helped innumerable people and the people in their support system cope with brain injury. The intent is to convey to you hope and coping strategies. We believe that persons with brain injury can respond to brain injury successfully. Note that we said "respond," not adjust, since we believe that this is an ongoing process, whereas "adjust" implies finality. Learning to respond is part of life and we are ardent believers in the capacity of persons with brain injury to respond.

You are not alone. Brain injury from trauma alone continues to impact about 1.5 million people each year. This dwarfs the number of new cases of AIDS/HIV, multiple sclerosis, spinal cord injury, and breast cancer, *combined*. Moreover, this number is probably low, as it does not include many active-duty service persons who have sustained acquired brain injuries while deployed overseas, particularly in Iraq and Afghanistan.

We wrote *Overcoming Grief and Loss After Brain Injury* to provide the best interventions for facilitating positive and successful responses to the losses of brain injury. It is meant to be a practical resource. The exercises and information within the nine Lessons focus on helping you learn about the injury from a personal perspective.

Our experience is that people with brain injury want to live productively and with purpose. We hope this book will help you address grief resiliently by engaging in a hopeful, positive manner toward your goals.

Janet P. Niemeier
Robert L. Karol

Acknowledgments

I have learned from many hundreds of my clients with brain injury how little there is out there in terms of practical resources to help people with brain injury and their families adjust to this complicated and challenging injury. I hope the book will provide a strong foundation of information and coping skills as well as a guide for not only clients with brain injury but their therapists who want to help them. Thanks to all of you for giving me the gift of sharing your experiences and selves for a little of your journey.

I am grateful and want to thank all of my mentors at Virginia Commonwealth University Health System Brain Injury Unit, Outpatient Neuropsychology and Rehabilitation Psychology Services, the Rehabilitation and Research Center on North Hospital First Floor at VCUHS, and in Egyptian. I have learned skills, patience, sensitivity, and empathy from you all. Without your modeling and support I would not have been able to reach this point.

My deep admiration goes to many wonderful colleagues tackling the difficult issues on the community front line where fragmented services for persons with brain injury lead you toward creativity, amazing advocacy, and self-sacrifice that I have noted and tried to emulate.

To the staff of Oxford, I am grateful for your confidence in us and support of this project which will hopefully help many persons and their families who did not ask for but are trying their best to live with this injury and its aftermath.

To my brother, Tim, and his family, Mary, Chris, Thomas, Chrystal, and the new generation represented by Lucas. I am proud of you all and grateful for your being out there in the world for me to love and as my family of supporters.

Most of all, thanks to my Richmond, Virginia and Ypsilanti, Michigan family—Dave, Carrie, Clay, Carolyn, and Patrick—who love and are with me no matter what. I could not do anything without you. Thanks to Raleigh for pointing out that it is important to take a break and play catch sometimes.

—JPN

Foremost in my thoughts as I wrote this book were the persons with brain injury and their families with whom I have worked over all of my years of practice. I have learned so much from them that I have shared with other people grieving their own losses. I have always explained to newly injured people that the role of the therapist is to be a conduit of knowledge from the past successes and setbacks of previous clients to newly injured people so that they can learn from the experience of others. Hopefully this book will bring their accumulated experience to many other people.

I also want to recognize all of my friends at the Brain Injury Association of Minnesota, my professional second home. They are all a great source of support and knowledge and their tireless work on behalf of persons with brain injury is heroic. While I could list everyone there, those most helpful with this book in particular were Breanna Berthelsen, Brad Donaldson, and Pat Winnick.

I want to acknowledge all of the great colleagues at my practice who have blessed me with their friendship and hard work. In particular, I want to recognize Drs. Nancy Carlson and Tom Kern who have been with me for years. They are loyal, dedicated, intelligent — and a source of very pointed humor.

There are also other people who work diligently on behalf of persons with brain injury. These include two physicians who deserve recognition: Drs. Robert Sevenich and Kenneth Britton. Both are smart, insightful, and caring. They have always had my back. Also due for praise are Beth Bohnsack and Mike Sandmann, great colleagues and confidants.

Furthermore, I want to acknowledge the staff at Oxford for their faith in us. They believed in the value of this book when we proposed it and they helped us make it a much better book.

I owe an unpayable debt of gratitude to Patricia Florio, my second grade teacher at Longfellow Elementary School in Teaneck, NJ. She saved me.

In the real world outside of work, Bradley, Daniel, Hilleary, and Meredith are special people who care deeply about other people. They are just getting started in changing the world. Look out.

My brother Michael is a kind and gentle person. We are bound by shared experiences. He is special and I love him deeply.

My mother, Rhona, is the source of my compassion and I am in wonder at the sacrifices she made on my behalf. I have learned to cope with my grief at losing her.

Finally, Gwen. Nothing I achieve is complete without her, this book included. My work, my life, my self requires her.

—RLK

Contents

Overcoming Grief and Loss After Brain Injury

Introduction

We recognize that you may have had little experience either with hospital rehabilitation or a community-based care system prior to your brain injury. Plus, when you seek help, unaware professionals may refer to your grief in a way that sounds like an illness by using clinical terms and tests. However, research now tells us that many emotional reactions could be normal grief.

In addition, while good work is now underway to find the best ways to address the needs of persons with brain injury, scholars and researchers have a comparatively new interest in acquired brain injury. Still, while there is more known now about the rehabilitation of brain injury because of this research and work, many clinicians who wish to meet the emotional needs of people struggling to respond to the losses of this devastating injury lack knowledge. This in turn leaves people with brain injury at a loss to find their emotional way. *Overcoming Grief and Loss After Brain Injury* was written to address your needs and the needs of your support system so that you can implement the best interventions.

It is meant to be a practical resource. The exercises and information within the nine Lessons will focus you on learning about your responses to your injury. You will be invited to relate each topic to your own injury experience, through questionnaires, exercises, and writing tasks.

The Lessons are organized in an order that illustrates a usual succession of concerns immediately following the injury and during later, post-acute periods. However, use your judgment as to what sequence you feel is best in completing the Lessons. You can work through the Lessons at your own pace. You do not have to complete all of a Lesson at one time.

The Lessons take into account that people will have a multitude of problems to address and many areas of concern. The intent is not to present an exhaustive list of treatments and interventions, but simply select the methods for addressing specific cognitive, social, behavioral, and functional problems related to brain injury that are supported by scientific research.

The rationale for the book includes the following concepts and beliefs about you that are evident in research and in experience.

- You and your family members will benefit from having information about brain injury and recovery.

- You will be more motivated to participate fully in even challenging rehabilitation tasks if you understand the purpose of the tasks and their role in achieving successful recovery.

- If you realize that your range of emotions and thoughts after injury are not unusual, you will be less likely to have stress or catastrophic reactions to changes in your skills and independence following injury.

- A comprehensive, informational book about adjustment after brain injury, which provides support and coping skills, will give you a head start in your recovery.

Goals of this book include the following:

- To provide you with information about symptoms, normal emotional and behavioral disruptions, and coping skills related to your brain injury

- To provide you with a structured, systematic, focused program of study

- To provide you with state-of-the-art treatment information related to enhancing outcomes for you

This book can be used as a stand-alone resource for you, or you may choose to work through the book with a therapist. The language and concepts and the stepwise pace of the exercises should allow you to complete the book on your own, if you so choose. This book is also intended to be a guide for family members, or other people in your life, providing families and others with insights into your coping, and with a specific Lesson for them (Lesson 7). Nevertheless, working with a professional can be helpful to gain additional insight and the process of study with a therapist should be enjoyable. If you have a therapist, there is a companion book, *Therapists' Guide to Overcoming Grief and Loss After Brain Injury*, for your therapist. You should be aware that no book can address the myriad of issues and situations that can arise, and the book does not replace the need for expert help when required.

Lesson 1

Brain Injury Facts, Realities, and Inspirations

Overview

The primary goal and intent of this Lesson is to assist you in identifying and understanding common symptoms and phases of recovery from brain injury, and that what you are going through is not unusual. This Lesson will use personal stories and examples, as well as the research-supported opinions of brain injury providers, to move you toward better post-injury adjustment. You will learn about common symptoms and causes of brain injury. You will also learn about the purpose of rehabilitation, the major players in the process, the roles of all members of the rehabilitation team, and the importance of acceptance and use of strategies for your successful recovery. The exercises and examples will help you identify the best outlooks and coping ideas for your long-term adjustment following brain injury.

Goals for This Lesson

- Learn about common causes and symptoms of brain injury

- Understand the stages of recovery from brain injury

- Learn about the major persons on your rehabilitation team

- Learn about the purpose of rehabilitation and your role in the process of getting better

The information in Lesson 1 will provide new understanding of the very common feelings and emotions that you may have been experiencing since your injury.

The comments in Box 1.1 are either made by clients with brain injury or reported by rehabilitation providers who seek to support you in your recovery from brain injury. The comments are heard or said by so many people, with injuries like yours, that it is important for them to be a part of Lesson 1. These are direct quotes from some of the 1.5 million or so persons in the United States who have brain injuries each year, and who lose abilities and independence as a result. As you can see, brain injury takes an enormous toll on many people in our country. Now look at Box 1.1 and read each quote carefully. As you review these quotes it may be reassuring to you to know that many of these people have gone on to do very well with support from their medical rehabilitation team, their family members, and friends, and from the consistent use of coping strategies.

Your Concerns and Feelings

Do you have any of the feelings and concerns expressed by persons quoted in Box 1.1? Try to identify any feelings or challenges you have had that are similar.

Box 1.1 Brain Injury Brings Changes, Feelings, and Questions

"I lost my mind, or at least half my brain!" *(Man, 35, hit by a car while walking)*

"I want to get back to work, but I can't remember anything." *(Woman, 41, fell off her horse)*

"I'm so angry that I lost my memory." *(Man, 31, was run over by a drunk driver while working on construction site)*

"I have lost so much time from work and away from my family." *(Man, 24, had a torn artery during a car accident, surgery to repair it, and then a stroke)*

"I am so frustrated! I feel so tired all the time; I lost all my energy." *(Woman, 74, fell and had bleeding in her brain)*

"It's scary. I don't feel like myself anymore." *(Man, 29, injured in a head-on car crash)*

"I am sad that I have lost so much time with my baby … where did it go?" *(Woman, 19, had stroke on the delivery table while having her first child)*

"I can't speak right." *(Man, 60, brain tumor)*

How did you get your brain injury? If you are not sure, ask someone close to you to tell you details about your injury. It may be that the cause of your injury has been experienced by many other people. Look at Box 1.2. The Box contains a list of the most common causes of brain injury. You may not understand or know about some of these causes. Notice whether the cause of your brain injury is on the list. If it is, you can see that you are not alone in your situation. If you are not sure about the cause of your brain injury, check with a family member, using the list. The main point is to realize that there are many in the larger community of persons around you with brain injury who have had similar experiences.

Now look at the questionnaires in Boxes 1.3 to 1.5. You may need to find a family member or caregiver who was with you at the time of your injury to help you fill in all the injury facts if you are not able to remember all of them. If you are reading this book as part of work with a brain injury therapist or counselor, the process of taking the questionnaires could be simplified by either having your caregiver present in the session or placing a telephone call to the caregiver during the session. While it may take a little time to complete the questionnaires, and you may need to get help writing your answers, there are two very important reasons to finish them. First, if you can

---

Box 1.2 Common Causes of Brain Injury

Motor vehicle accident	Unexpected surgical event	Sports injuries
Assault	Fall	War injuries to the head
Shaken baby episode	Heart attack sequelae	Stroke and aneurysm
Drug abuse	Drug/medication overdose	Bacterial infection
Toxic chemical exposure	Gunshot wound	Carbon monoxide exposure
Tumor	Near drowning episode	Metabolic disturbance
Encephalitis and meningitis	Lack of oxygen	Alzheimer's disease
Parkinson's disease	Multiple sclerosis	AIDS

become more aware of the facts about your injury and the feelings you are having about it, you will find it easier to choose the best steps to take toward recovery. Second, if you understand the purpose, process, and major players on the rehabilitation team, you will be much more likely to work hard and get the most out of it.

As you work through these exercises and questions, you may find it helpful to talk about your responses and feelings with a therapist, as well as friends and family you trust.

Box 1.3 Injury Facts Questionnaire #1: I Had a Brain Injury Because of... (circle all that apply)

Motor vehicle accident	Unexpected surgical event	Sports injury
Assault	Fall	War injury to the head
Shaken baby episode	Heart attack	Stroke or aneurysm
Drug abuse	Drug/medication overdose	Bacterial infection
Toxic chemical exposure	Gunshot wound	Carbon monoxide exposure
Tumor	Near drowning episode	Metabolic disturbance
Encephalitis or meningitis	Lack of oxygen	Alzheimer's disease
Parkinson's disease	Multiple sclerosis	AIDS

Other_____

Box 1.4 Injury Facts Questionnaire #2: Facts about My Brain Injury

When did the injury occur?	
Where did the injury occur?	
Where did rehab take place?	
How long was the rehab?	
Is more rehab needed?	
What problems are still there?	

How Is Your Family Doing?

Now we will take a look at the impact of brain injury on some often neglected members of the rehabilitation team—family members and caregivers of the person with the brain injury. Each of the main characters in the quotations below in Box 1.6 are struggling with the changes and challenges that come from having a close family member with a brain injury. These comments show how family members and significant others can also be touched by the losses associated with the injury.

Have you heard any of these comments from people you are close to, people who provided you with support and care in the early days of your injury? Family members and friends are often very important members of the rehabilitation team. They love to help and support the person with the brain injury. However, they sometimes lose sleep, miss work, worry, and are stressed out by trying to help their family members make progress in recovery from a very complicated injury or illness. It is important to remember them and thank them for their support. They are another reason for you to work hard in rehabilitation, proactively and consistently follow all the suggestions your therapists give you, and become as independent as you possibly can.

Reassurance and Help for "Invisible Symptoms"

One of the most challenging symptoms following brain injury is often invisible. The symptom of "unawareness" comes about from the confusing mismatch between a usually unchanged outward physical appearance and your mostly unseen cognitive and emotional changes related to the injury. Material in Box 1.7, as well as the story examples that follow, will help you understand this sneaky symptom. As you read through the examples, notice how unseen symptoms can lead to lack of awareness of your limitations. In addition, you can see from the stories that problems with self-awareness, which are very common after brain injury, can make it hard for you to get back to work and have satisfying relationships in your community and at home.

Brian's Story—A Success

Brian was driving home from an out-of-state business trip late one evening. The next thing he knew he was in a hospital bed with a headache. The strangers around him identified themselves as nurses or therapists. They all told Brian that he had been in a serious motor vehicle accident and was in brain injury rehabilitation. He struggled to fight crushing fatigue to organize his thoughts, think, and remember even a little of what had happened to him. He asked person after

Box 1.7 The Walking Wounded

In the 1980s and 1990s, several noted neuropsychologists began use of the term the walking wounded, to describe persons with even mild brain injuries. This term refers to the often "invisible" symptoms of the brain injury. Persons with brain injuries are often unchanged in their physical appearance. Without casts or bandages, what has been lost is often only apparent to those who are closest to them. The person with the brain injury may not realize these invisible symptoms exist. A brain injury symptom called "unawareness" may hide what the injury has caused for the person who has that post-injury symptom. The lack of awareness of changes caused by the brain injury can result in frustration for both the person and the people close to them. If the brain injury is the only injury from an accident or illness, and the person does not realize they have changed, much silent and unwitting suffering can occur as the person struggles to go back to work or home tasks. Read on to see some typical experiences of those who have sustained a brain injury. If you are a person who has had a brain injury, you may be surprised to notice some similarities between these stories and your own memories of injury and recovery. If you are someone concerned for a person with a brain injury, you may find some similarities between the experiences of your loved one and those of the persons described in this Lesson.

person, "Where am I?" "What happened to me?" When staff or relatives told him what happened, he soon forgot what they told him and had to ask again. He became irritated with those around him because they were having trouble understanding what he was saying for some reason. His family and the medical staff told him that a passing motorist had reported seeing his car in a gully. His car appeared to police to have drifted off the highway. He learned that his head struck the dashboard, resulting in a subarachnoid hemorrhage in the left side of his brain. Brian was determined to remember the cause of his accident. He asked everyone for clues, but no one knew. He got a nurse to find a version of the police report in his medical chart admission papers. It was agonizingly short on details. "Male, 40's, status post single car crash, found with LOC [loss of consciousness] slumped forward on dash of his vehicle, 2:45 a.m. Left forehead laceration. Male transported to trauma center via medical rescue helicopter."

As his thinking began to clear, Brian became aware of a weakness in his right hand and leg. He was annoyed as nurses and therapists told him not to get up without help, not to go to the bathroom without first calling them, that he couldn't have a drink of water until his swallowing test, and that he had to stay out of bed. When he tried to get up anyway, he was wobbly and had to grab furniture to avoid falling. One time he fell. Finding it hard to hide the frustration in their voices, staff members were constantly telling him not to get up or yelling, "Sit down!" At times Brian found himself wearing a cotton jacket that was tied to a chair so he couldn't get up. Staff would occasionally use soft arm bands to keep him restrained in his bed or chair, saying "it is to keep you safe." As he tried to ask questions or express his feelings and thoughts, he noticed that it was very hard to get his words to come out clearly. Brian's wife and son were overwhelmed, confused, embarrassed, and frustrated with him. Brian's wife and son treated him as if he were being rude or acting like a child. Though he could not figure out why, they seemed overwhelmed, confused, embarrassed, and frustrated by him. All Brian wanted to do was sleep, have people leave him alone, and find out what happened to him and why he didn't feel like himself anymore.

Brian's story and his symptoms of unawareness can be summarized in the following points.

- Brian's experience is quite common after a brain injury.

- Persons with brain injury often report that they feel at first like they are in a fog.

- Fatigue is frequently a constant companion.

- Speech may be confused, slurred, and faint. It may be hard to understand the speech of others.

- The brain injury can cause a range of typical impairments in thinking skills, especially memory and reasoning.

- If you have a brain injury, you may struggle to make sense out of your situation. You may feel restless, on an emotional roller coaster, and not as able to tolerate even minor frustrations. You can snap at those close to you.

- You may be unsafe because you do not realize your limitations.

■ Fear of loss of independence and control after brain injury can drive you to rebel against the staff and family who are trying to keep you safe.

The main thing to learn from Brian's story is that multiple problems can be caused by impaired self-awareness after brain injury.

Brian had the good fortune of finding several forms of help that became available for him as well as his family. Brian's story shows a typical recovery path.

His story and the rest of the Lessons in this book will clarify how persons with brain injury and their family members are able to find and access healing and helpful resources. Many people, for example, receive both inpatient and outpatient rehabilitation services following brain injury.

Hope and Healing

Brian's initial inpatient rehabilitation was provided by a team of specialists that included a physician, social worker, neuropsychologist, physical therapist, speech language pathologist, occupational therapist, recreational therapist, and nurse specialist. He was given medication temporarily to help him sleep better at night and stay awake and alert during the day therapies. He made excellent progress with his walking and was able to leave the hospital with only a cane for assistance with balance. His rehabilitation program included physical therapies as well as education. He spent at least one, and sometimes two sessions a day with the neuropsychologist, social worker, occupational therapist, and speech therapist learning about his injury as well as practicing memory and thinking strategies. The team of therapists also trained him to monitor and control his behavior consistently so he could be less impulsive, safe, and appropriate with others. Counseling was helping him, and his family, understand and accept the challenges resulting from his brain injury. His characteristic kind and caring ways were slowly returning to his daily interactions with family and friends.

Brian was fortunate to also receive outpatient rehabilitation. Many people, like Brian, transfer from inpatient to outpatient rehabilitation in a fairly short period of time—two weeks to one month. Like Brian, you could make great progress in inpatient brain injury rehabilitation, but you may still have some problems to work on. Outpatient therapy teams usually do a new assessment or evaluation of persons with the brain injury after they are discharged from the hospital and arrive in the outpatient rehabilitation center. The inpatient team often sends a report of your progress to the outpatient center, so the outpatient therapists can compare the findings of their new evaluation of your strengths and weaknesses. The outpatient team then sets new goals based on the new evaluation because these new goals best guide your next steps in recovery.

Brian's Story Continues

Over the next 12 months, a typical time frame for most persons following discharge from an inpatient brain injury unit, Brian's outpatient rehabilitation therapists began to get him ready to resume work. He was able to obtain a job through his state's department of rehabilitation services. A job "coach" went to work with him for a while to help problem solve any barriers to Brian's becoming a productive worker. With family support, and because he gradually became more aware of his challenges, Brian has managed to regain much of what he lost and is successfully relying on new ideas for coping.

Brian's story is a good illustration of what many people with brain injury experience during their initial recovery time, the first several months after injury. Brian and other persons like him, improve their self-awareness, so critical for making progress, because their helpers gently guide them toward realizing what they need to work on.

The Brain Injury Rehabilitation Team

Next, we will review the activities and major professionals in inpatient and outpatient rehabilitation in Box 1.8, the "Rehabilitation Team Members and Their Jobs." Even if you attended both acute and post-acute rehabilitation many months ago, the information may clarify the purpose of the rehabilitation process for you and hopefully renew your efforts to draw upon skills and knowledge you learned during that time. This will be especially true if you have trouble remembering much about your early rehabilitation experiences or, at that time, you were not as aware of what you needed to work on as you are now.

The information in Box 1.8 is meant to be a preliminary and brief overview. Lesson 3, "The Rehabilitation Hospital System: Staying Focused and Positive," will provide you with more detailed information and concepts about rehabilitation. However, for getting started in learning about rehabilitation, there are several important ways the information in Box 1.8 will help you get better. First, what you learn about the purpose and reasons for rehabilitation will help you participate more fully and get the most out of your hard work in any ongoing therapies. Second, if your rehabilitation is over, the information you gain from completing the reading and work of Box 1.8 will help you see how important your effort is for getting better. Finally, your renewed understanding of your role in making progress will make you more determined to consistently use strategies and information you learned during rehabilitation to help improve functioning.

Think for a minute about what you remember of your rehabilitation experiences. What were some of the great and no so great experiences? Are there any gaps or periods of time you do not remember about your days in rehabilitation? How did your experiences make a difference? What was your rehabilitation most focused on? As a result of this exercise in Box 1.8, you may realize that you did not experience all the forms of help or team members listed while you were in rehabilitation. You may express regret or a wish to obtain such services and a vision of how that would be helpful now. A physiatrist or therapist experienced in working with people who have brain injury could help you make a connection with available community resources that are within your ability to travel to and afford. If you are reading this as part of your work with a therapist, you can work together to receive the cognitive and behavior therapy that you now know you need.

Box 1.8 Rehabilitation Team Members and Their Jobs

Rehabilitation Team Member	I Know About or Worked with This Team Member	Circle All Skills and Needs the Team Members Helped You With
Nurse	Yes ___ No ___	Medications Bathing Toileting Changed bandages Taught me how to recover well
Occupational Therapist	Yes ___ No ___	Retrain upper body strength and flexibility Dressing Grooming Managing money
Physical Therapist	Yes ___ No ___	Retrain lower body strength and flexibility Balance Safety in moving around Pain and stiffness
Physician	Yes ___ No ___	Major and minor medical needs Prescribed my medications Finding me health care resources
Psychologist	Yes ___ No ___	Understanding and adjusting to my situation and changes in my abilities Helping my family adjust Listening and letting me talk about my feelings
Recreational Therapist	Yes ___ No ___	Balancing the work of rehabilitation with leisure fun Showed me how to be active after disability

Box 1.8 Rehabilitation Team Members and Their Jobs *Continued*

Rehabilitation Team Member	I Know About or Worked with This Team Member	Circle All Skills and Needs the Team Members Helped You With
Social Worker	Yes __ No __	Finding services and resources in the community Planning further rehabilitation Financial assistance
Speech Therapist	Yes __ No __	Language skills Memory Reasoning Swallowing

The following stories will illustrate the difficulties persons with brain injury may encounter when they are not able to obtain rehabilitation services or when their entry into rehabilitation is delayed. Rehabilitation services are valuable and those with brain injury who are fortunate enough to have them need to participate and work hard to take advantage of them. After each of the stories take time to think about the events and people involved. Write down your opinions. Think about what Pat, Audrey, their children, and John were feeling and how they were coping with their situations. Finally, try to decide if you have had similar experiences and feelings.

Pat's Story—Challenges and Despair

Not every person with brain injury is able to have rehabilitation. In addition to financial reasons, an incorrect diagnosis can occur, one that totally misses the existence of a brain injury. Let us look at the following story to see how a brain injury can go undiscovered with drastic consequences.

After seven months, Pat finally made an appointment to take her three children to see a therapist. She needed help with parenting. Since her car accident almost one year ago, family life had become chaotic. Everyday chores seemed overwhelming to Pat. Her ability to manage had been dwindling and she was losing her temper more and more frequently with the kids. She couldn't get the 6-year-old to sleep in her own bed. The 10- and 13-year-olds were fighting with each other and baiting the youngest until she cried. They all refused to do what she asked them to do. Her husband was also recovering from neck, back, and leg injuries, so could not manage the children well either.

Pat's return to work, eight months after the accident, brought the behavioral and parenting challenges at home to a crisis point. With the advice of a friend Pat made an appointment with a local family therapist. The psychologist took one look at the waiting room full of out-of-control children, the passive and bewildered mother, and asked Pat to come in first. During the interview, the psychologist began to ask a lot of questions about the accident. Pat reported what doctors, nurses, and family members told her, explaining to the psychologist that she herself could not really recall a thing. She and her husband were told that they were coming home from a New Year's Eve dinner at a local restaurant when their car was hit broadside by a pizza delivery truck. As a result of the impact, her husband's right shoulder pushed into her left chest, breaking eight of her ribs and collapsing a lung. Both of them were feared near death. They had to be cut out of their car and were rushed to a local hospital trauma center.

Doctors in the emergency room quickly sent Pat up to the operating room where surgeons worked to re-inflate her lung and remove her spleen. The final physician's summary stated that most of the couples' injuries were in their chest and extremities, and that Pat and her husband would eventually recover. Family members took care of the children for the three weeks that she and her husband were in the hospital and for the two months they were ambulating with crutches at home. Pat and her husband were in pain and on various pain medications for a long time. The youngest child was tearful, anxious, and clingy. She refused to sleep in her own bed.

Pat was very happy to return to work. However, Pat, once known for her organization and time management in running a busy household of five and holding down a demanding managerial job, did not seem to have any energy or skills anymore. Details began to slip through her fingers. Major mistakes became frequent, both at the office and at home. Dinner did not seem to get on the table regularly. The children were not getting to bed on time. All her husband wanted to do was take his pain medication and sleep. He had applied for and received disability insurance and was not able to return to work.

After talking with Pat and administering some cognitive tests, the psychologist finally met with the entire family. She referred Pat to a neurologist, reporting to Pat that the test results suggested that the accident may have caused a brain injury, perhaps not known or diagnosed at the time. Pat and her children were told about brain injury symptoms and given printed information from the Brain Injury Association of America (www.biausa.org). As it turned out, Pat was later diagnosed with a moderately severe anoxic brain injury caused by a lack of oxygen to her brain at the time of the accident. She was referred for and went through outpatient rehabilitation. She learned strategies for coping with her memory problems and was able to resume her job on a part-time basis. She improved her parenting skills, though she required parenting help with and counseling for her children. Fortunately, her family had the financial resources to provide the help she needed.

Audrey and John's Story

At 5 p.m. Audrey knew her husband was nearing home after one of his truck runs up the coast. Tonight she did not receive his usual CB-radio call telling her he was almost there. Instead a highway patrolman arrived to tell her John had been taken to a hospital about one hour away. She threw on her coat, called her mother to come watch their 6-year-old twins, and took off for the emergency room.

Audrey heard from the emergency room staff that a passing motorist notified police that John was driving slowly and weaving all over the road. John actually was able to radio his company dispatcher to tell her he was feeling sick, pull his truck over, and put on the brake, before collapsing on the steering wheel. Hospital staff worked to stabilize John. A scan revealed an aneurysm, a small "bubble" in one of the blood vessels in his brain, had burst. A team of surgeons operated to drain the blood, removing a piece of his skull to prevent further damage from swelling. Audrey was overjoyed to see her husband when they finally took John back to his room in Neuroscience Intensive Care. The helmet covering the exposed portion of his head was a constant reminder of how close a call this was.

John was quiet for a few days, receiving nutrition and medicine from tubes and IVs. Then he started to move restlessly. He would open his eyes when Audrey called his name but close them again quickly. "Does he still know me?" Audrey wondered. John's days and nights were mixed up. He was up at night and wanted to sleep during the day. The few words he spoke were scrambled or mixed up. Despite being told to leave his helmet on, he kept trying to take it off. He pulled out his IV twice. Audrey missed her twins but tried to stay with John at night, while her mother was at home with the children. She was exhausted during the day, trying to keep up with her sons. John was embarrassing her. He tried to grab the nurses and ask them for kisses. He was demanding and ungrateful toward Audrey. He pleaded for her to take him home and became enraged when she said she could not.

John's progress was slow, and he was moved to a nursing home for a time. His behavior improved, but he still acted like a child much of the time. Audrey was able to be home with her children more, but she missed her partner and spouse. Their finances were nearing collapse so Audrey took a part-time job. She was forced to learn about the banking and finances, and struggled to find out what she could about community resources for her husband's return. She fought her own depression, especially when friends and relatives told her "You should be grateful he survived!" It was difficult for her to be the loving, helpful wife when this man she married now seemed like a stranger.

Summary

These stories are about real persons and their families, and medical staff hear them often on the typical brain injury rehabilitation unit or outpatient mental health clinic. The symptoms, feelings, struggles, and losses experienced by Brian, Audrey, John, Pat, and their families are common markers of the beginning of the life-long journey of persons who have sustained brain injuries and their family members. With these and other stories in the Lessons ahead, you can see that many people share your same normal, and common brain injury problems and experiences, which are normal and common. The large number of persons with brain injury in your community and in the United States not only provides a network of support for you and others, it helps doctors and providers learn much more about this injury. Armed with knowledge about these common injury symptoms and problems, you will be better able to identify and ask for the training and information you need to continue a successful recovery.

Lesson 2

A New Sense of Self—Lost and Found

Overview

The purpose of Lesson 2 is to provide you with strategies and coping methods to help you work through your grief about your losses and changes resulting from your brain injury. Adjustment to post-injury changes and challenges, and coping with grief, can be more successful and tolerable when you are actively participating and working toward getting better. The material and exercises in Lesson 2 will help you identify particular problems from a range of common post-injury impairments in memory, attention, endurance, planning and organization, problem solving, communication, and relating to others. For example, you may have noticed, or others have told you that you have trouble managing your behavior or communicating effectively since your brain injury. Problems with behavior, speech, and processing are often described as the most limiting and socially isolating difficulties following brain injury.

Goals for This Lesson

■ Identify common brain injury challenges

■ Identify your specific challenges

■ Learn strategies for managing physical problems after brain injury

■ Learn strategies for managing impairments of attention, memory, problem solving, self-management of behavior, emotions and coping, and communication

Lesson 2 focuses on giving you specific tools for overcoming many very common injury challenges. In Lesson 2 you will find descriptions of a range of brain injury challenges, questionnaires to help you identify your own, and guided practice of techniques that will enhance your skills in these important areas of post-injury concern. Active and consistent efforts to try out these techniques will give you some steps toward improvement that will provide hope and encouragement, despite normal feelings of sadness about what has changed. There are many ideas, and working with an experienced provider will enhance your ability to learn all suggested coping methods.

Lost and Found

Persons with brain injury often say "I just don't feel like myself." They describe it as a strange feeling, a loss, and have trouble putting it into words. Many times this new sense of self does not go away. If you have a brain injury, have you had a sense of being different than you were before your injury? If you have this feeling, you are fortunate for two important reasons. First, brain injury experts actually know a lot about common symptoms of brain injury that are often the cause of that "different" sensation. Many of their suggestions for compensating for these symptoms will be presented in Lesson 2. Second, lack of self-awareness can be a huge problem after brain injury. If you already know what you have to work on, you are way ahead of the game. This self-awareness will help you select the strategies for improvement that you most need, and put them to use quickly.

What You Don't Know Can Hurt You

Not knowing how the brain injury affected you can make it hard for you to know what to do to feel more like yourself and on top of things again. Knowing about common injury symptoms will also help reassure you that you are experiencing normal symptoms for a person with a brain injury and will also allow you to take advantage of strategies and coping methods that can best help you progress in recovery, despite your being sad that things have changed.

No two people are alike. Every brain injury is therefore completely unique. People get better at different rates. Some people have mild brain injuries, while others have severe injuries. The biggest post-injury loss many face is poor balance and other physical changes. Others struggle with speech and memory problems. The change from good health to experiencing physical, language, and memory problems after a brain injury is almost always accompanied by normal loss and grief. Let's look at some examples.

Tim's Story

Tim fell off a roof when he was installing gutters and had a brain injury. Doctors told him that he made a good physical recovery and he was discharged from the hospital. Tim still feels tired most of the time, and barely has enough energy to get up, have breakfast, and watch television. He wonders why he is so tired. He worries that something is terribly wrong with him.

Jason's Story

At the garage where he is employed full time as a mechanic, a small part on a car engine broke off while Jason was testing the new spark-plugs he had installed. When his co-worker started the engine, the metal part went flying and into the front of Jason's skull, then his brain. Jason did not lose consciousness. He was discharged and sent home quickly from the hospital after his injury and the surgery to remove the metal piece. Jason's vision was blurry though, and he is still having trouble seeing. The sunlight makes it harder for him to see. He is worried about being able to go back to work.

Jane's Story

Jane was in a car crash. She didn't remember anything until she woke up in the hospital. It bothers her not to remember. She works as a waitress and she thinks she might have trouble remembering all the customers' orders. She is also having trouble sleeping at night. Jane worries that she is going crazy.

Fatigue, blurred or impaired vision, and memory problems are very common after brain injury. No one told Tim, Jason, and Jane about typical brain injury symptoms, so they began to feel hopeless and afraid. Tim was sad about losing his energy and endurance. Jason was experiencing a loss of vision that could affect his employment future. Jane knows she has a significant loss of memory and is grieving that. If you are experiencing any of these symptoms, you are likely grieving as well and may find the ideas for improvement in Lesson 2 helpful. Working on getting better by using strategies that work helps improve your outlook and gives you hope.

How About You? How Are You Doing?

The Brain Injury Symptom Questionnaire (BISQ) in Box 2.1 will help you identify many common injury symptoms you may be experiencing. Take the questionnaire, checking all items that are true for you. Try to be as honest as possible. If you are not sure, ask others if they have noticed that you have the symptom. The questionnaire is long because there are a large number of people with brain injury symptoms and they report many different kinds of symptoms in a range of combinations. As you read through the questionnaire, you should notice that your symptoms are not as unusual as you may have thought.

The list of symptoms in the questionnaire can be divided into three sections that represent three parts of recovery from a brain injury. Recovery from brain injury is part physical (**P**), part cognitive (**C**), and part emotional and behavioral (**EB**). The letters by the check boxes on the list show which type of symptom each item refers to. These divisions in the BISQ—that is, **P, C**, and **EB**—help group the ideas for improving according to type of symptom.

Notice how many symptoms you checked. Did you check more **P** symptoms, or **C** symptoms, or **EB** symptoms—or a mixture of all three? Everyone who has a brain injury is different, with different challenges in different symptom areas. If you can identify your own unique set of symptoms, you will be at a very important starting place. Once you know what you need to work on, you can choose the right strategies and ideas for recovery.

Box 2.1 Brain Injury Symptom Questionnaire: Since My Brain Injury I Notice I...

Get tired more easily	☐	P
Move more slowly	☐	P
Lose my balance	☐	P
Have a lot more headaches	☐	P
Am more likely to drop things	☐	P
Feel weaker	☐	P
Have more trouble falling or staying asleep	☐	P
Feel dizzy	☐	P
Have twitching muscles	☐	P
Have bathroom accidents	☐	P
Feel confused	☐	C
Misplace things	☐	C
Lose my train of thought	☐	C
Think more slowly	☐	C
Have trouble thinking of words	☐	C
Make more spelling mistakes	☐	C
Have trouble speaking clearly	☐	C
Have trouble listening	☐	C
Write slowly with messy letters	☐	C
Have trouble making decisions	☐	C
Get distracted easily	☐	C
Am more likely to forget what I do, read, say, or hear	☐	C
Am more likely to yell or curse	☐	EB
Am more restless and jumpy	☐	EB
Have less patience	☐	EB
Cry more	☐	EB
Want to be by myself more often	☐	EB
Am more grouchy	☐	EB
Have a hard time getting started on tasks	☐	EB
Hear others tell me I am not safe doing things alone	☐	EB

Notice the letters in parentheses next to the information and strategy sections. They are the same as those on the questionnaire you took. You can refer back to your BISQ and, using these letters (**P, C,** and **EB**), you can match your symptoms to the ideas offered for improvement.

Improving Your Physical Symptoms (P)

Fatigue and Restlessness

People with brain injury fall into three groups related to sleep and restlessness.

1. Some feel tired all the time. You may have drowsy periods during the day, even after a full night's sleep. You might complain about always feeling tired.

2. Others are very restless and have trouble sitting still. Staff and family members may be telling you to "slow down" or "wait for help before you get up."

3. Still other people with brain injury experience a combination of both kinds—you feel tired during the day because you have trouble sleeping at night.

You may identify with one of these groups.

Now look at "Coping with Fatigue and Restlessness After Brain Injury," Box 2.2. As you can see, there are several causes and aids for sleepiness, sleeplessness, and restlessness. Box 2.2 contains information about the causes of sleep and energy problems after brain injury on the left side, and ideas for improvement on the right side.

There are several reasons for disturbed sleep and energy after brain injury.

First, the actual injury and resulting changes in the brain are part of the reason that people have difficulty with either sleep or restlessness afterward. Since there are actual changes in the chemistry and structure of the brain from the injury, medications often work well to help with this. A doctor who is

Box 2.2 Coping With Fatigue and Restlessness After Brain Injury

Causes of Fatigue	Ideas for Improvement
Neurological changes	Medications, engage in any safe activity to bring on natural sleepiness, avoid doing too much at once
Pain	Medications, relaxation technique (3-minute chill-out)
Medications	Change in dosing
Worry	Relaxation techniques, positive self-talk, enjoyable social activities
Diet	Foods and beverages without caffeine, healthy food choices

aware of the needs of clients with brain injury will know best whether medication will help you, and what type you need, for how long, if you have this problem. The good news is that challenges with sleep and restlessness usually get better over time.

Second, people often have pain due to headache or injuries to their bodies from other injuries during the accident that caused their brain injury. The pain can keep you up at night, which results in drowsiness during the day. A brain injury physician is experienced in choosing a pain medication that will reduce discomfort without making a person drowsy. It is very important to report pain if you have it, and to take any medication prescribed as instructed. As all injuries heal, the pain will most likely get less intense.

A third cause of sleep/restlessness problems can be the medications themselves. Some medications that are needed for behavior or pain can also have side effects. The best choice in dealing with sleepiness due to medication is to ask your doctor if there is a different dosing pattern than can help. For example, if you normally take your medication in the morning, and think it makes you sleepy, you should ask your doctor if you can take it at night or split the dose, taking half in the morning and half in the evening. You certainly want to be sleepy at night!

▪ Fourth, worry can interfere with sleep and behavior. There are many realities to deal with after a brain injury. Bills are still coming in. You may worry about getting back to work to support yourself. You may worry about your bills. However, worry actually does little good. There are options and solutions for crises involving housing, finances, family issues, and getting back to work. Social workers are members of rehabilitation teams and community service centers that provide help with this. You might ask your doctor to recommend a social worker, or seek advice at the local Brain Injury Association Chapter near you. You can look this up in the phone book or on the internet at www.biausa.org under your state. Other Lessons in this book will provide more information about getting emotional supports as well as many links and information about community-based aids for adjustment and return to work.

A technique is described in Box 2.3 that is designed to help you relax and improve your ability to sleep well or become less restless—even while you deal with all of these post-injury challenges and issues day to day. Try to find some quiet time, by yourself, to practice this. Practice this "3-Minute Chill-Out Technique" about two times a day until you really feel like you are getting some benefit.

▪ A fifth cause of sleeplessness and restlessness can be diet. Try to make good dietary and nutritional choices, and avoid highly caffeinated drinks or foods not part of any special diet you may require to maintain good health, such as a diabetic diet.

Balance and Dizziness

Problems with balance and dizziness can result in falls and additional injury, which can result in lengthening your recovery time after brain injury. In the typical inpatient or outpatient rehabilitation center, it is usually the physical therapist (PT) who works with persons who have balance problems after brain injury. A person with a brain injury will get the most benefit from physical therapy for balance problems if they try their best to come to therapies on time

Box 2.3 The 3-Minute Chill-Out Technique

Close your eyes.

Take a deep breath, let it out slowly, saying "relax" to yourself.

Now take another deep breath, hold it, and notice the tension in your chest muscles.

As you let your breath out slowly, say "relax" to yourself.

Afterward, notice how much more relaxed your chest muscles feel.

Take another deep breath, hold it, and notice the tension in your chest muscles.

As you let your breath out slowly, say "relax" to yourself.

Afterward, notice how much more relaxed your chest muscles feel.

Now keep your eyes closed and imagine you are lying on a warm, sandy beach, listening to the waves roll in and out.

Now notice your breathing is smooth and even, just like the sound of the wave.

A wave rolls in, you breathe in.

A wave rolls out, you breathe out.

In, out.

In, out.

Feeling very relaxed.

Use this technique anytime you feel stressed, wake up and are unable to get back to sleep, are in pain, or feel overwhelmed.

and work as hard as they can, even if they are tired or have some discomfort. Dizziness can be caused by the injury itself, visual disturbances, inner ear problems, and can cause nausea and distraction. Physicians can help with medication changes, an eye patch, or may recommend increased rest breaks to improve dizziness and reduce risk of falls. Some behavioral strategies will also help, including slowing down when moving around, taking time to get up from a sitting position, and trying not to get distracted when moving around. If you have balance or dizziness issues try to focus only on moving, rather than moving while talking, watching television, or trying to look at something out the window.

Lower and Upper Body Weakness and Gait Problems

As with balance and dizziness, steady work on all the exercises and activities planned by your physical therapist will improve your lower body strength and gait. The PT will know how much should be done, how soon, and how fast. In addition, the occupational therapist (OT) is usually the rehabilitation team member who provides therapy to strengthen the upper body. The OT can also help you practice real daily activities like dressing, grooming, and work-related tasks.

Improving Your Cognitive Impairments (C)

Confusion

Confusion is usually seen as an early brain injury symptom, but can also occur if the person with the brain injury is tired or having to deal with more than one task or difficulty at a time. Consistent use of aids for memory such as calendars, schedules, a dry erase board with daily information, and a memory log will help keep you on top of daily tasks. Your family and caregivers can help by calling your attention to these aids, or assisting you in consistent use of memory aids. Posting all of the aids in highly visible places is also a big help. Family members and friends can provide verbal reminders, or cues, until you get better at remembering to use them on your own. When confusion continues to be a problem, contact your brain injury physician who can recommend some medications that are known to improve this.

A Strategy to Reduce Confusion

Consistent use of the "Daily Information Sheet" (DIS) in Box 2.4 is also recommended for reducing confusion. Transferring or copying the sheet onto a dry erase board will allow you to erase entries and reuse the space many times without using lots of paper. Each day you will use one copy of the DIS. At the beginning of each day, write your answers to each of the questions on the left side. Place the sheet on your refrigerator or some other very visible place to help you stay aware of the facts of your day.

Box 2.4 Daily Information Sheet (DIS)

Fill Out Each Day	
The month is ?	
The day is?	
The date is?	
The year is?	
What will I be doing?	

Problems with Attention/Concentration

Distractibility is a frequent problem after brain injury. Have you noticed that you have difficulty focusing or concentrating? Poor concentration is a frustrating brain injury symptom for a number of reasons. People need to be able to pay attention to be safe, learn, remember, follow instructions vital to recovery, manage money, and do daily tasks. Box 2.5 suggests some strategies helpful for improving attention.

Memory

Memory problems are some of the most challenging and universal after brain injury. There are several kinds of memory—short term, delayed, long term, and prospective—and these are often what your rehabilitation team focuses on to help you get better. The good news is that most people keep long-term recall following brain injury. For example, can you remember your mother's name, address if you have lived in the same place for many years, or the name of the last school you went to? Most people can recall these things because they have known them for a long time. Remembering new information, like names of people you have not known very long, is more difficult after brain injury. Problems with delayed memory and prospective memory can disrupt your daily routine and work. Delayed memory refers to the ability to recall what happened, what you read, what you heard, and what you saw several minutes to hours later.

Box 2.5 Strategies for Improving Attention After Brain Injury

■ **Reduce distractions.** If working on your bank statement, for example, put your chair toward the desk or table, away from a window. Turn off all electronics such as TVs, radios, etc. Ask others to help you by being quiet as you go about your own activities. If you have small children, plan to have someone help you watch them while you try to focus on critical daily tasks, or get the children settled doing something they like before you start working.

■ **Tell yourself to "Pay Attention!"** We all talk to ourselves. That is a fact. You can "coach" yourself by using this very human trait. Simply say "Pay Attention" or "Focus" to yourself to coach yourself toward improved attention.

■ **Try to get enough rest at night.** Keep regular hours whenever possible. Go to sleep when most folks do. Avoid caffeine, heavy foods, overly stimulating (scary!) movies or shows, etc. before bed. If you have pain that keeps you up at night, ask your doctor for help so you can rest.

■ **Don't try to do too much at once.** This is especially true if you have gait or balance problems, or if you have to concentrate to express yourself verbally.

■ **If you have trouble with right or left visual attention.** Turn your head and eyes together to both the left and right, like a lighthouse. Think very consciously about bringing your chin all the way over to your shoulder, first your right shoulder, then your left shoulder, and back again. Practice this while walking around, to improve safety and visual memory.

Prospective memory is being able to remember to follow through with something you scheduled or planned at an earlier time. It is frustrating to forget information, and sometimes dangerous! Boxes 2.6 and 2.7 provide ideas for compensating for deficits in both these types of memory.

Problem Solving

This section on problem solving is really about several thinking abilities that are sometimes disrupted by brain injury—reasoning, self-awareness, self-management, memory, attention. All these areas,

Box 2.6 How To Improve Memory After Brain Injury

- **Repetition.** Say information (names, items on shopping list, class information, therapists' instructions, addresses, phone numbers) 3 to 4 times. You can repeat by hearing, doing, writing, saying, and reading things. It may take many practices of 3 to 4 times each practice to remember something.

- **Write things down.** Pick a notebook, pad of paper, clipboard, day planner, or make a "memory notebook" page to organize and keep information in one place. A memory notebook should have the following components to work well: daily sheets with the correct date, a copy of your daily schedule, a copy of a weekly schedule, and a list of important telephone numbers (especially physicians and helpers; emergency numbers).

- **Use schedules.** Hour by hour with room to write is best.

- **Use calendars.** Put on the wall or refrigerator with a magnet. Have spaces you can write in and tie a pencil to the spine of the calendar.

- **Use electronic helpers.** Computers, watches with date, personal data assistants (PDAs), memo cards, audiotape recorders, email, pagers, GPS or navigation devices for the car. (Beats trying to remember directions!)

- **Use other people.** Pick someone you trust with a good memory to remind you of things like taking medicines, doctors' appointments, when bills are due.

- **Work on improving your attention, a building block of memory.**

- **Work on improving organization, a building block of memory.**

- **Mnemonics.** Use the letters of a word to help you remember. The NAME strategy, described in Box 2.7, is a mnemonic device. It helps you recall names you want to remember. Practice this with people you would like to get to know better.

any of which can be impaired after brain injury, have to work together for people to be able to solve problems of daily living. Lesson 2 will help you with problem solving in two ways. The information in Lesson 2 will improve your understanding of this skill area. Second, you will learn to use strategies for improving your

Box 2.7 Sample Mnemonic: The NAME Strategy

N — Notice the person.

A — Ask for their name.

M — Mention the name 3 to 4 times to yourself. "Jerry, is your Dad named Jerry too? Is Jerry short for Gerald? Do you spell Jerry with a G or a J?"

E — Exaggerate something about the person to yourself that stands out, so it will serve as an image you associate with their name.

problem-solving skills for all kinds of problems. People can have several possible challenges to problem solving after a brain injury. Some of the skills they need for problem solving, such as memory, attention, and decision making, may be impaired. Brain injury can also make it more difficult for you to think of more than one solution to a problem. The SOLVE strategy, presented in Box 2.8, is a strategy that can help make the process of problem-solving easier and more productive. The SOLVE strategy is like the NAME strategy for memory described earlier. Each letter stands for a step in the strategy. Consistent use of this step-wise, clear approach will improve your ability to effectively solve problems.

Let's look at the example in Box 2.9, as a way of demonstrating how the SOLVE strategy can work for you.

Now practice more on your own. Think of a real problem to try out further use of the SOLVE strategy. Take a blank piece of paper. Write "SOLVE" down the left side of the paper in large letters, leaving about two inches between the letters. Now try to fill in each blank next to each letter using the format above.

Improving Your Emotional, Social, and Behavioral Problems with Recovery Strategies (EB)

This section of Lesson 2 will help you improve emotional, social, and behavioral skill areas that can be disrupted after brain injury.

Box 2.8 The SOLVE Strategy to Improve Problem Solving

S — Situation

O — Options

L — Listen to others

V — Voice a choice, pick an option

E — Evaluate your outcome

Executive Functioning: Behavioral Self-management

After brain injury many people have difficulty with self-awareness and self-regulation. As a result, friends and caregivers may see you as unsafe, and tell you to "slow down" or watch you closely. Friends and family may be insulted when the person with the brain injury blurts out inappropriate comments without thinking. People with

Box 2.9 Using the SOLVE Strategy

Sample Problem: You have three bills to pay and no income since you have been out of work for about three months during rehabilitation. You have got enough money to pay one, but all are due. Let's use the SOLVE strategy to solve the problem.

S — Three bills due but only enough money for one is your situation.

O — Your options include:

1. Pay the oldest bill, and calling the other 2 companies to work something out over time.

2. Pay a portion of each bill, promising to keep on paying something each month.

3. Wait another month.

L — Ask someone good with finances whom you trust to help you think through each option, and who will listen to your opinions.

V — You "voice a choice" and decide to pay a portion of each bill.

E — The companies accept your partial payments and your promise to keep on making regular payments; you evaluate and decide that you solved your problem well!

brain injury may find this unwanted supervision or reactions to their behavior very irritating because they are adults and want to be independent. However, the brain injury makes it difficult for them to realize that they are acting in an unsafe or rude manner. Unfortunately, the brain injury often changes what is safe for the person to do, and the person may yet have healed enough to be aware of this. Sometimes it takes a fall, and further injuries, for the person with the brain injury to realize that things are different. How about you? Have close friends and family told you that you are moving too fast, are unsafe, or rude? If you think you may have these kinds of problems, you would probably do well to improve your self-management. You can avoid taking chances with risky or socially inappropriate actions and improve your self-management by using the "Be Your Own Coach" (BYOC) strategy.

"Be Your Own Coach"

Everyone has had or has been a coach at one time or another in their lives. What are the main jobs of a coach? If you said either "tell the players what to do," or "say positive and encouraging things to the players," you are correct. The BYOC strategy is very simple. If you function as your own coach, and use the strategy, you will tell yourself what to do—before you do it—and talk to yourself in positive ways. Jim's story will help illustrate how the BYOC strategy can work.

Jim's Story

Jim was serving as pitcher in a baseball game and took a line drive to his head. He was unconscious and later testing at the hospital revealed a brain injury. While Jim recovered in the hospital, his family and therapists noticed he was very impulsive. His parents watched him like a hawk. They made him mad because they followed him around, even to the bathroom! They just thought he was moving too quickly and were worried. Jim got fed up and had some heated arguments with his parents. The family was referred to a neuropsychologist who showed Jim how to coach himself, to tell himself "Stop, think, plan" every time he got ready to do something. This self-coaching gave Jim a few seconds more, a few seconds to avoid jumping up so quickly that he fell or tripped. In time, Jim's parents trusted him to function alone as his control of himself improved using the BYOC strategy. They relaxed as Jim began to more safely take charge of his own life again.

Can you think of some situations where, if you had used the BYOC strategy, you might have avoided unpleasant consequences? Try the strategy to improve your own self-management. Remember, the trick is to tell yourself what to do before you do it.

Improving Social and Emotional Functioning

After brain injury, many people tend to blurt out inappropriate or rude comments, get too personal with questions and remarks, and have problems with remembering facts that are important for keeping a relationship going. Any one or all of these problems can put some distance between you and the people you care about or the people you would like to meet and get to know. You may find that is it also more difficult to manage strong feelings since your injury. Having angry or tearful outbursts can also put a strain on relationships. In a nutshell, self-control, memory, and communication, which can all be more difficult for the person with a brain injury, are very important ingredients in getting along well with others. The BYOC strategy can help prevent injury but can also help you maintain the kind of self-control needed for all types of relationships. If needed, getting help from a physician who is experienced with treating people with brain injury can also help in terms of getting medication for controlling intense feelings and behavior problems.

Reread the parts of the Lesson that relate to coping with emotional ups and downs. There are many helpful ideas and discussions in this Lesson, as well as in Lesson 4 and others to come, about feelings following brain injury and how to cope successfully with these. Having emotional ups and downs is normal after brain injury. Positive self-talk and motivation to achieve doable goals are ways to reduce the intensity of the lows and work through your grief about your losses and changes.

Remembering the Important Things for Relationships

Lesson 2 has provided multiple ideas for improving memory. These can be useful not only for recall of daily information, but all can be applied to improve relationships with friends and family.

For example, if you are worried that you might forget a friend or family member's birthday, or an anniversary, you could use a combination of the calendar and writing things down as memory strategies. You can write important dates on your calendar and place it in a very visible place. As you turn the calendar pages, with the passage of months, you will be reminded by your own notes! The SOLVE strategy can be used for working out conflict with others in a productive manner, something that can be difficult after brain injury. If you work together with your friend, family member, or partner, and use the SOLVE strategy described earlier in this Lesson, you may reduce conflict and make progress toward improving your relationship. Make extra SOLVE practice sheets. Pick a practice example like: you want your friend to go to the movies with you, but you are tired and want to stay home. Work through the steps to see your options and possible solutions.

Effective Communication

Brain injury often makes clear communication a challenge. There are problems with being understood by others, understanding what others say, keeping up with the topic in a fast moving group conversation, talking too much or too little, and with listening to others without interrupting. Think about your own talking and listening skills. Are you dealing with challenges? The table in Box 2.10 presents ideas for improving communication. Communication between people involves talking, listening, and nonverbal communication. Box 2.10 contains ideas for improving each of these parts of communication in order to improve your relationships and interactions with others.

Consistent use of the guidelines for communication in Box 2.10 will be helpful in getting your points across while listening to others so they know you are interested.

Summary

Lesson 2 has covered many ideas and strategies for coping with some common symptoms after brain injury. The information and ideas will guide you to look closely at yourself, and take stock of all your

Box 2.10 Ideas for Improving Communication After Brain Injury

Talking	Listening	Nonverbal Behavior
Slow your speech down if you have trouble getting your words out.	Always let the other person talk more than you do.	Don't stand too close.
Avoid discussing or asking personal things.	Make good eye contact, but don't stare.	Don't touch unless you know them really well or they ask you to.
Don't interrupt.	Turn off loud radios or TVs when others talk.	Don't scratch or pick at anything!
Don't talk on and on about your injury.	Wait until the other person is finished before you talk.	Don't clench your fists.
Use the person's name frequently.	Ask the other person questions to show interest.	Keep a pleasant, friendly facial expression.
Avoid cursing or telling off-color jokes.	Don't answer your cell phone when someone is talking.	Don't walk or turn away as you talk.

strengths and weaknesses that accompany you as you continue to get better. While loss is a part of brain injury, you will be ahead by being able to clearly identify what you have lost. At first, this may not make sense. You might think "I feel sad and angry about losing my ability to speak clearly." However, your grief about this loss can be more tolerable if you actively use coping ideas to overcome what is now more difficult for you to do, and take comfort in the strengths you still have. Knowing your unique pattern of strengths and weaknesses will help you benefit more from rehabilitation therapies and be more likely to consistently use the specific coping strategies you need. Use of the many tools and ideas in Lesson 2 will help you move through your grief and toward a more satisfying, independent, and less stressful life after injury.

Lesson 3

The Rehabilitation Hospital System: Staying Focused and Positive

Overview

The preceding lessons introduced the idea that challenges are a normal part of coping after brain injury and that there are concrete strategies you can use to make life easier. For many persons with brain injury, the coping process begins during rehabilitation. Lesson 3 addresses how to be most successful during the time in the hospital. If you never went to a rehabilitation hospital or have already left, you can adapt relevant parts of this Lesson to better understand the health care players you may still encounter, or want to seek out, in a clinic situation and how they function.

In this Lesson, you will learn how the rehabilitation system works. You will see how it differs from other health care that you may be familiar with, and what your role should be. You will gain insight into who to ask for help during rehabilitation for various issues. Reading this Lesson will enable you to maximize the benefit you get from rehabilitation.

Goals for This Lesson

- To better understand the rehabilitation hospital system
- To learn the differences between traditional and rehabilitation care
- To be more comfortable during rehabilitation
- To understand your family's response to your rehabilitation

"This is so different from the acute hospital unit."

"My surgeon said I was going to be fine, but here they keep discussing compensating for deficits."

"My therapists are talking about discharge, but I don't feel ready."

"I don't know why they want me to see a psychologist."

"As a family member, I feel lost; everyone is focused on my loved one, but I have worries, too."

Professionals who work to help rehabilitate persons with brain injury are aware that rehabilitation is a unique experience for you and your family. Still, you may be surprised to learn that most people receiving rehabilitation have sentiments similar to those expressed above. To prepare you for the emotions that you may experience during rehabilitation, it is important to understand what rehabilitation is and is not, and what it can and cannot accomplish. By better understanding rehabilitation, you will find that you can have more say in how your care proceeds.

The Nature of Rehabilitation

Rehabilitation differs from most other health care in two fundamental ways:

- The goal of rehabilitation is to facilitate your functioning and teach you how to make up for deficits, but not to cure injury or illness.

- Rehabilitation requires your participation.

These two simple statements are at the heart of all rehabilitation. Yet, if you fail to appreciate their implications, you will be frustrated with the care you get.

Let us explore the meaning for you of the first statement. Most health care compared to rehabilitation strives to accomplish different goals in treatment. In much of traditional health care the goal is to cure or fix the problem:

- Physicians set broken legs to fix the break.

- Wounds are cleaned and sutured so that they heal.

- Medications cure infections.

In contrast, most of the symptoms that bring people to rehabilitation are not curable: brain injury is a classic example. Professionals are unable to "fix," or cure, brain injury. Hence, the goal of rehabilitation is to facilitate brain function so that your deficits are reduced or so that you learn to use other parts of your brain to "compensate"— that is, accomplish the same task in a different manner—for the injured part of your brain.

Rehabilitation may be the first phase of treatment after your injury in which your health care providers discuss recovery in terms of deficit reduction and compensation rather than curing you. This may be as shocking to you as it is to most people. The contrast in this regard between acute treatment and rehabilitation treatment can be overwhelming.

It may be the first time you realize that your recovery may be incomplete. You and your family may even have been told at the initial acute hospital that you were "going to be fine." Many people with brain injury and their families breathe a sigh of relief upon being told this, taking the words literally to mean "complete recovery."

To address any confusion you should be clear about your expectations.

Exercise

What were you told about your recovery before coming to rehabilitation? (e.g., "You are going to be fine.")

_____

_____

_____

What did you think that meant? (e.g., "I will have a complete recovery.")

_____

_____

_____

_____

_____

It is important to understand acute professionals. They often are involved in saving lives and they do miraculous work. However, many acute-care professionals:

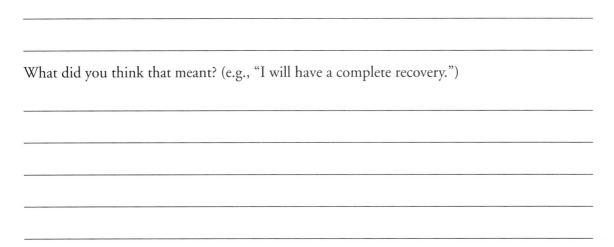 Are trained to fix and cure problems.

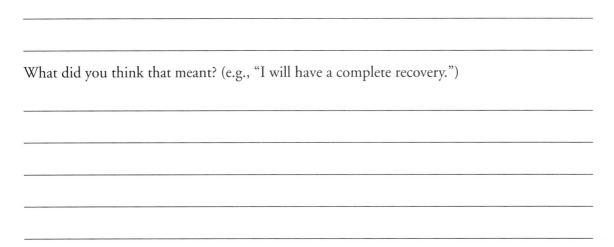 Usually give out good news.

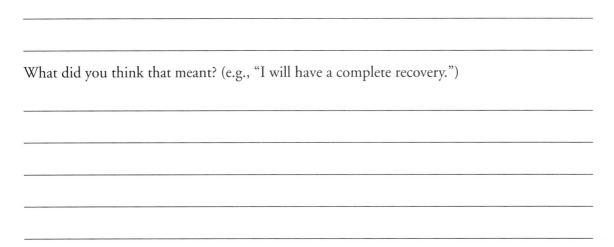 May be emotionally unprepared themselves to tell you news that might distress you.

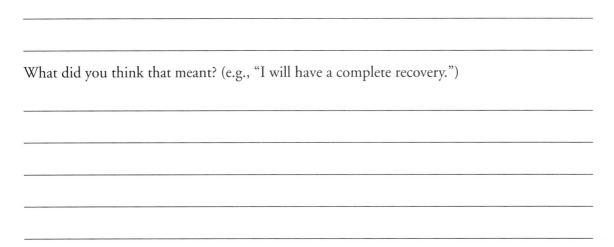 Mean you will likely be able to "walk and talk," though without specifying how well, when they say "You are going to be all right."

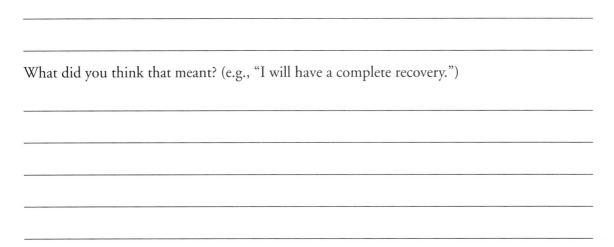 Do not follow people for years to know how their predictions play out and they may believe you will be fine.

When your rehabilitation team begins to discuss limitations it can be very disappointing. Many people even complain that they have been told that everything will be ok. You may experience considerable disbelief or even anger when your rehabilitation team disagrees with the messages you have been given in acute care.

Be assured that they will work to minimize your eventual limitations, sometimes called residual deficits, and maximize your abilities, but some problems may be permanent. You should make sure your team knows about your feelings and about the messages they are giving you, so you can work together more effectively.

Exercise

How did you feel when you first heard your rehabilitation team talk about residual deficits, incomplete recovery, or limitations?

_____

_____

_____

_____

_____

What would you like your rehabilitation team to know about your expectations?

_____

_____

_____

_____

_____

Who on your team are you going to tell about these feelings?

_____

_____

_____

_____

Despite being told that your recovery may not be complete, you should *not* take this to mean that you should abandon hope. Your attitude and effort can greatly affect your eventual abilities. This brings us to the second difference between traditional care and rehabilitation, and it can be the source of amazing outcomes!

YOUR EFFORT MAKES A HUGE

DIFFERENCE IN YOUR OUTCOME!

Your effort makes a huge difference in your outcome. Really. In other aspects of health care this is less true.

- When you take medications, so long as you take the medications as prescribed, the chemistry of the pill requires little from you.

- When you have surgery, you passively lie on the surgical table.

However, in rehabilitation you must work to get results. Your therapists will require you to do physical structured activities to improve your strength, coordination, balance, sensation, etc. They will need you to do guided mental tasks to enhance thinking, reasoning, concentration, memory, and awareness.

The job of therapists is to:

- Design retraining and compensation techniques for you.

- Provide you with the right exercises – physical and mental – to retrain you or teach you to compensate.

- Guide you in doing these exercises.

- Give you "homework" to practice between treatment sessions.

It is important to note that they are not doing things *to* you in the manner that medications or surgery do.

If you find yourself surprised by rehabilitation therapists pushing you to more thoroughly participate during rehabilitation, it may be because the results depend on your effort. A physical therapist in an Intensive Care Unit may move your leg to help maintain its movement, but a physical therapist in rehabilitation is more likely to teach you exercises to perform to strengthen your leg.

The differences between traditional care and rehabilitation are summarized in Box 3.1.

Box 3.1 Differences Between Traditional Care and Rehabilitation

Traditional/Acute Care	Rehabilitation
You are passive.	You must be active.
Therapists do things to you.	Therapists teach you to do things.
Your participation makes less difference.	Your participation makes a great difference.
The goal is to cure.	The goal is to improve.

You should be aware of the *potential* for limitations and engage in rehabilitation to reduce them. Stay positive and focused on doing the best you can in rehabilitation to improve your results. It is valuable to write down your new goals for rehabilitation, other than being cured, in terms of improvement and limiting residual problems.

Exercise

What goals do you want to work on in rehabilitation?

_____

_____

_____

_____

What limitations do you most want to reduce?

_____

_____

_____

_____

_____

What limitations are you ready to live with if you cannot eliminate them?

_____

_____

_____

_____

_____

How will you remind yourself every day that your effort and motivation in therapy can make a huge difference?

_____

_____

_____

_____

The best advice from experienced rehabilitation professionals is to maintain hope, work as hard as you can to achieve your vision of recovery and fulfill that hope, while planning to make necessary life changes, if you must. Do not put all of your eggs in one basket: believe–have faith and avoid giving up. But be realistic–plan for various outcomes.

Emotional Help During Rehabilitation

The preceding section may have been very difficult to read. You may have found that it challenged your previous concept of your expected care. You are normal if you find that confronting your existing concepts is distressing.

The good news is that you are not alone. Centers that specialize in rehabilitation typically include psychologists as part of your treatment team. In fact, it is often routine that *everyone* sees a psychologist because the process of rehabilitation is so challenging.

Seeing a psychologist is recognition of how emotionally challenging it can be to have a brain injury. It does not imply that you are weak or mentally ill. Rather, grief is normal, but people tend to handle significant life changes better when they can discuss them with others.

Your psychologist can act as an expert source of information and can give you perspectives garnered from having listened to other people with brain injury. Explorers going into the unknown used scouts who had been there before; your psychologist is your emotional scout, having learned which ideas work for persons with brain injury and which ones increase distress: your psychologist knows the emotional landscape of brain injury, just like a scout knows physical geography. Use your psychologist to emotionally prepare yourself for your journey into the unknown turf of rehabilitation and brain injury.

The psychologist may come to visit you early during your rehabilitation:

- This is to establish rapport and to learn about you.

- This provides a head start on helping you cope in the future, if you find that rehabilitation and brain injury are overwhelming.

- It helps the psychologist know you, so that the psychologist can assist your family members who may need support themselves.

You may also be offered follow-up visits after discharge since the process of grieving often extends beyond rehabilitation. Of course, you and your psychologist may decide that you are coping adequately with little professional support and minimum help is necessary. Still, it is wise to maintain contact should this change in the future.

In addition to the rehabilitation team psychologist, there are other providers who can help you with emotional coping. You may find that you emotionally connect with lots of team members: physicians, nurses, therapists, chaplains, social workers, etc. Avail yourself of the guidance and knowledge of your whole team and blend perspectives to fit your needs.

It may be helpful to write down concerns you want to discuss with your psychologist so that you do not forget them. You can use the form in Box 3.2.

Getting Comfortable in Rehabilitation

At first, you may find that it is difficult to stay positive when you first arrive on the rehabilitation unit. You are in an unfamiliar environment with people you do not know. It is common for people to feel uncertain and worried.

In such circumstances you may seek to apply your own familiar routines only to find that the rehabilitation center has its own procedures. It is all right to discuss with your providers how you like things done so as to feel reassured. Many rehabilitation processes are flexible, and your team should strive to meet your desires. However, some procedures are set to accommodate everyone in the rehabilitation program or to maximize your recovery, and there may be less flexibility for those procedures.

Exercise

What routines do you usually follow? (e.g., time you wake up and go to sleep; time you take showers—morning or night; food preferences; clothing preferences; etc.)

_____

_____

_____

_____

Which of these are you flexible about?

_____

_____

Box 3.2 Log of Issues/Concerns/Emotions To Discuss with the Psychologist

Date	Issue/Concern/Emotion

_____

_____

_____

Which of these will distress you if you have to change them?

_____

_____

_____

_____

_____

Have you already encountered changes which are distressing you?

_____

_____

_____

_____

If you are unhappy about the rehabilitation routine, talk with your staff (i.e., nurses, therapists, psychologist, social worker, physician).

Also, certain items will give you a better sense of control.[1] Most rehabilitation centers will provide you with written material that can help with this. Ask for a:

- Schedule of therapies and unit activities

- List of your team members, their jobs, and their phone numbers (you may also want to ask for their business cards)

- Memory notebook or day planner to record your activities so that you can recall what you have been doing in treatment and

---

[1] Note that you are also entitled to various items by law, such as a Patient Bill of Rights, etc. Many of these are typically posted on your rehabilitation unit. If you want a copy, ask your social worker for a copy of any legally mandated material.

can establish a sense of continuity, which will make you feel more in control

- Copy of visiting hours

- Visitors' log book so that family and other visitors can write entries; you can review these after they leave to extend their emotional support

- Calendar for your room

- Hospital map

You can use the form in Box 3.3 to remember to ask for the items listed above, and you can use the form in Box 3.4 to write down the names of your team members.

Many of the concerns that this Lesson covers can also be addressed during family conferences. Rehabilitation centers usually will schedule periodic meetings with you, your family, and your team to make sure that they attend to any issues you and your family may have. The team will also tell you concerns they have.

Box 3.3 Request Reminder Checklist

☐ Schedule of therapies and activities

☐ List of team members

☐ Memory notebook

☐ Visiting hours

☐ Visitors' log book

☐ Calendar in room

☐ Hospital map

☐ _____

☐ _____

☐ _____

☐ _____

Box 3.4 List of Team Members

My Name:_____

Hospital:_____

Floor:_____

Unit:_____

Room:_____   My Room Phone Number:_____

Team Member Position	Name	Phone
Physiatrist (Rehabilitation Physician)		
Rehabilitation Psychologist		
Neuropsychologist		
Psychiatrist		
Neurologist		
Internist		
Physical Therapist		
Occupational Therapist		
Speech Pathologist		
Recreational Therapist		
Chaplain		
Dietician		
Pharmacist		
Social Worker		
Case Manager		
Patient Advocate		
Nursing Staff		
Nursing Staff		
Nursing Staff		
Nursing Staff		
Nursing Staff		

Box 3.4 List of Team Members *Continued*

Nursing Staff_____

Nursing Staff_____

Other Team Members_____

_____

_____

_____

_____

_____

_____

However, do not wait to voice your worries, or your hopes, to your team. In fact, your team may hold staff-only meetings more frequently than family conferences. Ask when the staff meetings or rounds are held. It is often useful to pose questions to your team before those meetings so that all of your team members can confer on how best to meet your needs.

Wanting to Leave the Rehabilitation Center

As rehabilitation proceeds, insecurity may still remain. You may be worried about how you are doing or how far you will progress. ASK! Insecurity increases in an information vacuum. As you proceed through rehabilitation, hopefully your sense of security will increase. Therapists, nurses, and others will become more familiar.

Yet, one large doubt may remain: "When will I be discharged?" This question can have two opposite meanings:

- "How soon can I go home?"

- "You can't discharge me; I'm not ready to go home!"

If you experience either of these sentiments, you are having natural reactions to rehabilitation.

Understanding Cognitive Treatment

You may feel that rehabilitation treatment, particularly the cognitive therapies to improve memory and reasoning, seem silly; the exercises look childish. This can stem from the fact that on the surface the tasks appear like childhood games or activities.

Yet, typically the therapists are trying to stimulate certain parts of the brain. Some of these simple appearing tasks do that because they require use of specific brain areas, whereas complex tasks utilize broad areas of the brain. (In the real world you use your whole brain, but if therapists only gave you real-world activities to do, there would be less attention paid to areas of difficulty.) Actually, a combination of specific brain tasks and application to real-world activities is most common.

Still, even many of the real-world activities that therapists focus on may seem like they are below your level of functioning before your injury. It is hard to work on things that you knew how to do before and that you thought you were done learning to do: you learned them in the past when you were younger and it can be frustrating to cover the same ground again.

Nevertheless, therapists need for you to show them you can do things now, not just that you could do them before your injury. Otherwise, you risk the therapists assuming you actually have skills that may have been affected by your injury and you will leave rehabilitation without abilities you need. It is difficult to spend time in your life relearning things, particularly thinking skills, but it is wise to take advantage of the time in rehabilitation to get as much back as you can.

Responsibilities at Home

Another reason for possible frustration with hospitalization is that there are real-world responsibilities you feel driven to get back to handling: paying bills, returning to work, repairing things in your house, etc. Moreover, you may be annoyed with your rehabilitation team because they seem to attend insufficiently to your concerns about those things. The likely reason for their focus on treatment rather than your life before your injury is that they believe your brain is not yet capable of handling these responsibilities *well*.

They may be protecting you from prematurely attempting tasks that their data about you, and their experience working with people before you, indicate will go poorly. While it can make you very angry, it is wise to remember that your team's insistence that you continue in rehabilitation reflects their desire for you to do well *after* discharge.

Sometimes to protect you therapists will

- Prohibit an activity (e.g., driving)

- Insist on your being supervised after discharge

- Advise a delay in returning to work (so you do not get fired because you returned too soon before your full skills were back)

- Stay in the rehabilitation center so that you *succeed* when you do return to the real world

Think of it as a positive sign when your team wants you to continue in treatment because it means that they believe you can benefit and get even better. A couple of more weeks in rehabilitation may mean a much easier time for the rest of your life; after all, when you are 90 years old looking back on your life you probably will not regret having worked a few weeks less now because you are in rehabilitation, but you may regret not having taken advantage of treatment that was available to you that could have made your life better.

Trusting Expert Advice

Finally, irritability with having to stay in the rehabilitation center may reflect your misperceiving the extent of your injury. It is difficult to see one's own memory, judgment, or reasoning problems. Your brain may appear fine to you. For example, it may tell you that you are recalling everything because it fails to realize how much it forgot!

However, your therapists and family may see the problem. Trusting your rehabilitation team in such circumstances is crucial, but it is difficult to trust these professionals who you have only known briefly. Perhaps the best way to consider this situation is think of them as experts who you have hired to advise you about cognition (i.e., thinking, reasoning, memory) and the implications of problems in these areas.

You trust experts you barely know – if at all – all of the time: an airline pilot, the people who built the bridge you drive over, the elevator manufacturer, etc. It seems harder in rehabilitation because your own cognition seems like something you should be the expert about – in contrast, you know you can't fly an airplane – so you have less faith when the rehabilitation team gives you information that is contrary to what your own brain tells you. Still, next time you look at a big jet liner think about this: Does your brain *really* tell you that great big metal thing will *fly*?

The Flip Side: Worried About Leaving Rehabilitation

Eventually your team will tell you it is time to leave. You may feel panic. Surprisingly, the rehabilitation center may have become a source of comfort. Everyone accepts you. You see other people addressing difficulties similar to yours. Everything is physically accessible (e.g., doorways, bathrooms, counter heights). There are nurses to help with activities of daily living. However, the real world can be a scary place.

Again, the issue is trust. Your caregivers want you to succeed. Tell them if you feel that you will have needs after discharge that they have inadequately addressed. If you are afraid, tell them that too. Part of handling brain injury is to acknowledge the range of emotions that you experience as you pass through rehabilitation.

Discuss your worries early, rather than waiting until the last minute. If they know your concerns, therapists will often arrange for practice experiences for the things you are concerned about (e.g., outings with therapists outside of the hospital or therapeutic passes to go home to family). Make sure you or your family keep a log to return to the therapists of successful activities that you attempt during passes, and the hurdles you encounter while on passes that need addressing. You can use the form in Box 3.5.

Box 3.5 Pass Activities Log

Name: _____

People you went on pass with:_____

Date of pass: _____

Was it an overnight pass: Yes [ ] No [ ]

Describe successes / Describe hurdles with:

Social/Recreational Activities

1._____

2._____

Transportation/accessibility

1._____

2._____

Taking medications

1._____

2._____

Basic routines (Meals, bathroom, bathing, dressing, Etc.)

1._____

2._____

Emotional/behavioral issues

1._____

2._____

Other

1._____

2._____

Remember, too, that once you go home the rehabilitation center does not vanish. You can always come for an appointment to get advice. In truth, it is best to schedule some automatic follow-up visits with your rehabilitation physician, psychologist, and therapists before discharge. Typically at discharge, you will receive discharge instructions that include follow-up visits and appointments for ongoing therapy. You can use the form in Box 3.6 to record your follow-up visits.

Box 3.6 After Discharge Follow-up Appointments

Date	Time	Professional	Address	Phone

Don't forget to bring a list of your medications with you to appointments. Write down questions you may have before coming and bring the list with you. Bring your memory notebook/day planner with you to write down recommendations during the visit.

Families Who Are Involved

Family members may experience unique challenges during your rehabilitation. It is important that you realize the role your family can play in your rehabilitation and be comfortable with their involvement.

One factor that confuses family members is that rehabilitation rarely proceeds without starts and stops. Ideally, every day would be better than the preceding one. In reality you may have setbacks. On any given day, you may look as you did a few days, or even weeks, ago. Factors such as a poor night's sleep, a stressful day, poor appetite, etc., may affect you more than you might expect or more than such things would have influenced you before your injury. Brain injury can change your sensitivity to these influences.

For your family members trying to discern progress, days in which you do poorly can be traumatic. They are often keenly aware of fluctuations in your abilities. In such cases you can encourage your family to seek reassurance from your treatment team so that they can understand which fluctuations they should accept as part of natural variations during rehabilitation and which symptoms ought to be of concern. If your family understands the natural process of rehabilitation, you may feel less pressure if you have an off day—so long as it is just a day once in awhile.

It is best if you feel comfortable with your family talking with your team because they may detect changes worth noting for your team. Your family knew you before your injury and they may be closely monitoring your status, so they may detect changes before your team. Consultation between your family and your team can help both do the best job for you.

Families Who Are Struggling To Understand

On the other hand, your family may struggle to accurately perceive your capabilities. This is true even when you are putting forth your best effort. For example, if you have trouble with initiation (e.g., starting activities, realizing you should do something, making plans), your family may sometimes believe you are lazy. This typically reflects that your family is trying to understand your behavior as if you did not have a brain injury. Of course, you can be lazy *and* have a brain injury, but other reasons may apply for your behavior due to your brain injury. Your family is probably unfamiliar with reasons for your behavior that are rooted in brain injury and your family may express disappointment with you.

In general, such emotions, while honest, are counterproductive. They lead everyone down a path of distress, guilt, or shame that might be avoided. Open discussion about the reasons for these feelings, including disclosures about your effort, their expectations, and your history before injury, can help avoid hurt feelings. If you believe your family is struggling to understand how hard it is for you to put forth your best effort, then you could suggest they talk with your team.

Similar problems can arise in regard to cognitive functioning. Your family may relate that your deficits are typical for you—"He always had a poor memory" or "She was never good at drawing" or "Math was never his strong suit." Any of these statements may, in part, be true. Nevertheless, therapists determine whether you have cognitive difficulties by using extensive databases to judge your performance and are looking at variations greater than those found in people without injuries—beyond what would be normal variations of being good or bad at something prior to having an injury.

Your family may report that they see no change from before your injury, despite reports by therapists to the contrary. Differences in viewpoint arise most commonly in regard to memory functioning.

- The discrepancy often occurs because of the complexity of memory functioning. Brain injury usually affects memory for new information, whereas memory for more distant events is sometimes spared. When therapists assess new learning they detect deficits, but when your family discusses events in your life from before the injury you seem fine.

- Families sometimes word questions to you that imply the correct answer and they provide enough information in the question so that you can answer.

- Sometimes you answer questions with a "yes" or "no," appearing to be accurately recalling, whereas you are just responding to the information cue they gave you.

- Family members may accept a partial answer, filling in the missing information, assuming you really knew the full answer. They assume you knew more than you said!

All of this can lead to great misunderstandings. Frustration between you, your family, and your team can begin because everyone has a different perception of your abilities. It would seem, therefore, that the best advice to help you and your family to cope is to quickly recognize when you and your family disagree about your functioning or when there is a difference with your team. Then, information should be exchanged so that everyone is working from the same foundation.

Summary

Brain injury is an emotional experience. It can induce fear, worry, depression, anxiety, hopelessness, disbelief, mistrust, frustration, anger, guilt, despair, and grief. Rehabilitation can, at its worse, increase these feelings, or, at its best, lessen them. Rehabilitation can be a period of reassurance, hope, belief, trust, growth, renewal, and faith. It is normal to grieve during (and after) rehabilitation; it is natural to experience a sense of loss and it is typical to see new possibilities in your future. Be assured that you may experience a range of emotions, all of which are normal.

Lesson 4

Emotional Responses to Brain Injury—
Reclaiming Grief

Overview

The primary purpose of Lesson 4 is to inform you about the many different emotional responses that are possible to experience following injury. In Lesson 4 we will also return to Brian's, Pat's, and John's stories from Lesson 1, this time using them as supplements for some guided exercises about emotions after brain injury. As we review the stories from Lesson 1 that describe experiences of real individuals with brain injury and their families, we will focus more on the feelings, struggles, and losses that each of them experienced. You will notice how these emotional responses are common markers during the journey of persons who have brain injury.

Goals for This Lesson

- Identify and accept your own feelings and worries related to your brain injury experience and recovery

- Improve self-management of feelings and worries related to your brain injury

- Adopt a positive view of your post-injury emotions and concerns

- Understand the complexity of coping with brain injury

Loss Is a Part of Having a Brain Injury

Before beginning the stories, consider Box 4.1 (a reproduction of Box 1.1 from Lesson 1).

Notice, in Box 4.1, that some of the words and phrases are bold-faced.

These boldfaced words and phrases represent common losses and emotions identified by persons from all ages and walks of life who have had a brain injury. Notice that people are reacting emotionally to a sense of having lost time with people they cared about, and for lost jobs, lost their ability to remember things and do activities or use abilities that meant so much to them. If you are a person with a brain injury, think about losses you have experienced as a result of your injury and the feelings that go with the losses.

As you work through Lesson 4, you will learn that while persons with brain injury are about 3 times more likely than persons without to develop depression, normal grief over losses experienced because of the brain injury can also explain sadness during recovery. Lesson 4 will provide you with information about how to know whether the emotional and behavioral reactions you are having are normal, or whether you should seek help in coping so that you can continue to make progress in your recovery.

Losses due to the brain injury and attempts to cope with them are often made more frustrating because of common problems with thinking, memory, language, and coping that also result from the brain injury. Of course, persons recovering from any injury or disability can encounter coping problems. However, brain injury is very different from other disabilities because the coping is done with a brain that is injured. A person who has a spinal cord injury copes using a brain that is intact.

There can be consequences from trying to cope with an injured brain. For example, a person with brain injury may not communicate well with the friends and family that they depend on for their recovery and return to the community. In addition to ideas in Lesson 2 about cognitive strategies, this book will help you overcome some coping pitfalls, making it more likely that your coping will be effective. Look back at Brian's hurdles, in his story from Lesson 1, to notice how he overcame these challenges. Notice the bolded words in italics. These words and phrases will help you identify all the losses and feelings that Brian and the people trying to help him were experiencing in the aftermath of his injury.

Revisiting Brian's Story

Brian was driving home from an out-of-state business trip late one evening. The next thing he knew he was in a hospital bed with a headache. The strangers around him identified themselves as nurses or therapists. He had been in a serious motor vehicle accident and was in brain injury rehabilitation, he was told. He ***struggled to fight crushing fatigue*** to organize his thoughts, think, and remember even a little of what had happened to him. He asked person after person, "Where am I?" "What happened to me?" When staff or relatives told him what happened, he found that he soon forgot what they had told him and had to ask again. He ***became irritated*** with those around him because they were having trouble understanding what he was saying for some reason. His family and the medical staff told him that a passing motorist had reported seeing his car in a gully. His car appeared to police to have drifted off the highway. He learned that his head struck the dashboard, resulting in a subarachnoid hemorrhage in the left side of his brain. Brian was determined to remember the cause of his accident. He asked everyone for clues but no one knew. He got a nurse to find a version of the police report in his medical chart admission papers. It was agonizingly short on details. "Male, 40's, status post single car crash, found with LOC (loss of consciousness) slumped forward on dash of his vehicle, 2:45 a.m. Left forehead laceration. Male transported to trauma center via medical rescue helicopter." As his thinking began to clear, Brian became aware of a weakness in his right hand and leg. *He was annoyed* as nurses and therapists told him not to get up without help, not to go to the bathroom without first calling them, that he couldn't have a drink of water until his swallowing test, and that he had to stay out of bed. When he tried to get up anyway, he was wobbly and had to grab furniture to avoid falling. One time he fell. Finding it hard to hide the *frustration in their voices*, staff were constantly telling him not to get up or yelling, "Sit down!" At times Brian found himself wearing a cotton jacket that was tied to a chair so he couldn't get up. Staff would occasionally use soft arm bands to keep him restrained in his bed or chair, saying "it is to keep you safe." As he tried to ask questions or express his feelings and thoughts he noticed that it was *very hard to get his words to come out clearly*. Brian's wife and son treated him as if he were being rude or acting like a child. Though he could not figure out why, *they seemed overwhelmed, confused, embarrassed, and frustrated by him*. All Brian wanted to do was sleep, have people leave him alone, and find out what happened to him and why *he didn't feel like himself anymore*.

Symptoms and Trials

Brian's experience is quite common after a brain injury. Persons with brain injury often report they feel at first like they are in a fog. Fatigue is frequently a constant companion. Speech may be confused, slurred, and faint. It may be hard to understand the speech of others. The brain injury can cause a range of typical impairments in thinking skills, especially memory and reasoning. Persons with brain injury thus *struggle to make sense out of their situation*. They may *feel restless, on an emotional roller coaster, and not as able to tolerate even minor frustrations.* They can snap at those close to them. They may be unsafe because they do not realize their limitations. *Fear of loss of independence and control* can drive them to rebel against staff and family who are trying to keep them safe.

Fortunately, before the end of our story, help becomes available in several forms for both Brian and his family. We continue Brian's story to show a typical recovery path. Brian's story, and this book, will also make clear how persons with brain injury and their family members can find and access healing and helpful resources. Many people, for example, receive both inpatient and outpatient rehabilitation services following their brain injury.

Hope and Healing

Brian's initial inpatient rehabilitation was provided by a team of specialists including a physician, social worker, neuropsychologist, physical therapist, speech language pathologist, occupational therapist, recreational therapist, and nurse specialist. He was *given medication temporarily* to help him sleep better at night and stay awake and alert during the day therapies. He made excellent progress with his walking and was able to leave the hospital with only a cane for assistance with balance. His rehabilitation program included physical therapies as well as education. He spent at least one and sometimes two sessions a day with the neuropsychologist, social worker, occupational therapist, and speech therapist learning about his injury as well as practicing memory and thinking strategies. The team of therapists also trained him to monitor and control his behavior consistently so he could be less impulsive, safe, and appropriate with others. *Counseling was helping him, and his family, understand and accept the challenges* resulting from his brain injury. He was becoming more aware of what he needed to work on. His characteristic kind and caring ways were slowly returning to his daily interactions with family and friends.

Brian was fortunate to also receive outpatient rehabilitation. Many people, like Brian, transfer from inpatient to outpatient rehabilitation in a fairly short period of time—two weeks to one month. Like Brian, they make progress in inpatient brain injury rehabilitation, but may still have some problems to work on. Outpatient therapy teams usually do a new assessment or evaluation of the person with the brain injury. They often have a report from the inpatient team. So the outpatient therapists compare their new findings with the old report to get an accurate picture of the client's current skills and abilities. The outpatient team then sets new goals based on the new evaluation because these new goals can then reflect the next steps in recovery. Over the next 12 months, a typical time frame for most persons following discharge from an inpatient brain injury unit, Brian's outpatient rehabilitation therapists began to get him ready to resume work. He was able to obtain a job through his state's department of rehabilitation services. A job "coach" went to work with him for a while to help problem solve any barriers to Brian's becoming a productive worker. With *family support*, Brian has managed *to regain much of what he lost* and is successfully relying on new ideas for coping.

Learning from Brian's Story

What does Brian's story tell us about emotional responses following brain injury and coping effectively? We see that he was annoyed, frustrated, and afraid. He had to work very hard not to give in to being tired. We also notice that his family was having normal feelings related to the changes in their lives resulting from Brian's brain injury and his injury-related behavioral and cognitive problems. Brian chose to really work hard in rehabilitation, taking advantage of every opportunity to get training and help. Brian's strategy, his positive outlook, his coping choice of sticking with rehabilitation and work, in spite of his being tired and frustrated, and his wonderful family support really paid off. He was able to work again and have a satisfying life situation, even though he still has ups and downs.

Looking Back at Pat's Story: Challenges and Despair

After seven months, Pat finally made an appointment to take her three children to see a therapist. She needed help with parenting. Since her car accident almost one year ago, family life had become chaotic. Everyday chores seemed **overwhelming** to Pat. Her ability to manage had been dwindling and she was **losing her temper** more and more frequently with the kids. She couldn't get the 6-year-old to sleep in her own bed. The **10- and 13-year-olds were fighting with each other** and baiting the youngest until she cried. They all refused to do what she asked them to do. Her husband was also recovering from neck, back, and leg injuries, so could not manage them well either.

Pat's return to work, eight months after the accident, brought the behavioral and parenting challenges at home to a crisis point. With the advice of a friend Pat made an appointment with a local family therapist. The psychologist took one look at the waiting room full of out-of-control children, the **passive and bewildered** mother, and asked Pat to come in first. During the interview, the psychologist began to ask a lot of questions about the accident. Pat reported what doctors, nurses, and family members told her, explaining to the psychologist that she herself could not really recall a thing. She and her husband were coming home from a wonderful New Year's Eve dinner at a local restaurant when their car was hit broadside by a pizza delivery truck. As a result of the impact, her husband's right shoulder pushed into her left chest, breaking eight of her ribs and collapsing a lung. Both of them were feared near death. They had to be cut out of their car and were rushed to a local hospital trauma center.

Doctors in the emergency room quickly sent Pat up to the Operating Room where surgeons worked to re-inflate her lung and remove her spleen. The final physician's summary stated that most of the couples' injuries were in their chest and extremities, and that they would eventually recover. Family members took care of the children for the three weeks that she and her husband were in the hospital and for the two months they were ambulating with crutches at home. Pat and her husband were **in pain** and on various pain medications for a long time. The **youngest child was tearful, anxious, and clingy.** She refused to sleep in her own bed.

Pat was very happy to return to work. However, Pat, once known for her organization and time management in running a busy household of five and holding down a demanding managerial job, **did not** *seem to have any energy* or skills anymore. Details began to slip through her fingers. Major mistakes became frequent, both at the office and at home. Dinner did not seem to get on the table regularly. The children were not getting to bed on time. All her husband wanted to do was take his pain medication and sleep. He had applied for and received disability insurance and was not able to return to work.

After talking with Pat and administering some cognitive tests, the psychologist finally met with all of them. She referred Pat to a neurologist, reporting to Pat that the test results suggested that the accident may have caused a brain injury, perhaps not known at the time. Pat and her children were told about brain injury symptoms and given printed information from the Brain Injury Association of America (www.biausa.org). As it turned out, Pat was later diagnosed with a moderately severe anoxic brain injury caused by a lack of oxygen to her brain at the time of the accident. She was referred for and went through outpatient rehabilitation. She learned strategies for coping with her memory problems and was able to resume her job on a part-time basis. She improved her parenting skills though she required parenting help with and counseling for her children. Fortunately, her family had the financial resources to provide the help she needed.

Learning from Pat's Story

What can we learn about losses, emotions, and successful coping after brain injury from Pat? Pat had to wait a long time to get reassurance about what she was feeling and experiencing because doctors did not notice her brain injury right away. She and her family members were overwhelmed, worried, and confused about her daily mistakes and coping problems. We see that Pat had anger and frustration. She did not understand what was wrong with her and took out her frustration on her children. The children reacted with misbehavior and anxiety. Pat trusted her instincts and sought help. She was referred to a professional who knew about brain injury symptoms and challenges. The professional gave Pat and her family the information and recommendations they needed. Finally, Pat started on the right path to recovery. She and her family were able to work back toward a better life together, despite Pat's brain injury. Information, professional support and guidance, and use of helpful coping can lead to improvements and progress even if a person gets a delayed start in dealing with a brain injury. Pat's love of her family, trust in her instincts, and her discovery of a professional skilled and knowledgeable in helping persons with brain injury were the primary factors in dealing with her losses and emotions in a successful manner.

Revisiting Audrey and John's Story

At 5 p.m. Audrey knew her husband was nearing home after one of his truck runs up the coast. Tonight she did not receive his usual CB-radio call telling her he was almost there. Instead a highway patrolman arrived to tell her John had been taken to a hospital about one hour away. She threw on her coat, called her mother to come watch their 6-year-old twins, and took off for the emergency room.

Audrey heard from the emergency room staff that a passing motorist notified police that John was driving slowly and weaving all over the road. John actually was able to radio his company dispatcher to tell her he was feeling sick, pull his truck over, and put on the brake, before collapsing on the steering wheel. Hospital staff worked to stabilize John. A scan revealed an aneurysm, a small "bubble" of one of the blood vessels in his brain, had burst. A team of surgeons operated to drain the blood, removing a piece of his skull to prevent further damage from swelling. Audrey was *overjoyed to* see her husband when they finally took John back to his room in Neuroscience Intensive Care. The helmet covering the exposed portion of his head was a constant reminder of how close a call this was.

John was quiet for a few days, receiving nutrition and medicine from tubes and IVs. Then he started to move restlessly. He would open his eyes when Audrey called his name but close them again quickly. ***"Does he still know me?" Audrey wondered***. John's days and nights were mixed up. He was up at night and wanted to sleep during the day. The few words he spoke were scrambled or mixed up. Despite being told to leave his helmet on, he kept trying to take it off. He pulled out his IV twice. Audrey *missed her twins* but tried to stay with John at night, while her mother was at home with the children. She *was exhausted during the day*, trying to keep up with her sons. *John was embarrassing her.* He tried to grab the nurses and ask them for kisses. He was demanding and ungrateful toward Audrey. He pleaded for her to take him home and became *enraged* when she said she could not.

John's progress was slow, and he was moved to a nursing home for a time. His behavior improved, but he still acted like a child much of the time. Audrey was able to be home with her children more, but she missed her partner and spouse. Finances nearing collapse, Audrey took a part-time job. She was forced to learn about the banking and finances, and struggled to find out what she could about community resources for her husband's return. *She fought her own depression*, especially when friends and relatives told her "You should be grateful he survived!" It was difficult for her to be the loving, helpful wife when this man she married now seemed like a stranger.

Learning from John and Audrey's Story

What can we learn about losses, emotions, and successful coping after brain injury from John and Audrey's story? John was not very aware of his behavior for some time, and as is often the case, his family had difficulty coping with his injury-related changes. As time went on medication, counseling, rehabilitation therapies, and hard work made the difference. We also learn that patience, acceptance, and focus on those blessings that are available are critical for making progress in recovery and readjustment after a brain injury.

Now we will look more closely at the range of normal emotional responses to brain injury. In Box 4.2 you will read about the many feelings experienced after brain injury by both the person who has the brain injury and their family members. Disabilities resulting from brain injury are like ripples in a pond when you are trying to skip stones. From that one event, ripples keep moving outward, touching all aspects of your life. The stone hits the water—the injury happens—and the effects spread out over time and relationships. A person can easily feel overwhelmed, sad, confused, afraid, grief-stricken, and defeated. Everyone reacts differently to changes in how they act, look, speak, eat, eliminate, feel, and think. Each person's injury is different. Each person's recovery has a different time frame and course. There are many different ways an injury can affect each person's day-to-day functioning and the people within their social network. You will likely have a range of fluctuating feelings of various intensities throughout your recovery and beyond. Use of the strategic coping methods and techniques outlined in Lesson 4 will help you overcome these common challenges and move forward in recovery.

Box 4.2 Normal Feelings After Brain Injury

If you are a person with a brain injury: Whether you have lost the use of your arm, memory, legs, speech, or vision, brain injury is bound to have a great impact on your life and feelings. The last thing you may remember before the accident or illness was being at work, school, or at home. Perhaps after being in a coma for weeks, you found yourself in a hospital. In a minute, you went from total independence to possibly having to wait for someone else to help you take care of even your most basic bodily functions. You may have been, or may still be, in tremendous pain. You may be wondering why you no longer feel like yourself. You may wonder who that "self" is now. Feelings and emotions may flow with worrisome speed and unpredictability. It may be frightening to see that those closest to you appear confused about how to help you figure things out. The good news is that all of these feelings and experiences are common and reported by almost all people who have experienced a brain injury.

If you are a family member, partner, or friend of the person with a brain injury: Many persons close to those who have sustained a brain injury report that they face their own significant changes and challenges in the wake of the injury. The following are some examples of common difficulties. First, family members frequently describe their own emotional roller coaster. Relief and gratitude for the survival of their loved one can quickly become sadness, fear, or even anger when they notice some unpleasant changes in the personality and behavior of the person they nearly lost. Second, it may become clear all too soon that the role of the primary wage earner in the family may be too difficult for the person with the brain injury to resume. A spouse or partner who never handled the family finances may now have to scramble to learn in order to avoid financial ruin following rising medical expenses

Box 4.2 Normal Feelings After Brain Injury *Continued*

and no income. Third, when the persons with the brain injury lose the capacity to take care of themselves and to make decisions, both their marriage and family can come close to falling apart. Adult children from a prior marriage, for example, may enter the picture and try to take the primary role in managing their parent's situation, ignoring the parent's new spouse. Finally, family members and friends can feel a loss of intimacy when nurses must now provide most of the physical care for their spouse or partner.

Good News: There are several pieces of good news that this Lesson, and the entire book, presents. First, most the emotions you are having are grief-related and normal for individuals and their family members who have losses associated with brain injury. That is not to say that recovery and coping are easy. In this Lesson we will tell you how to know when your symptoms and behaviors are becoming disruptive and self-defeating to the point that you should seek help. Second, the Lessons will guide you toward coping adaptively and show you how to avoid adjustment pitfalls in the wake of your losses. Finally, this and other Lessons in the book will provide information about finding and accessing supportive resources.

Normal Feelings After Losing Functions and Skills

For most everyone who has experienced a disability, the losses and changes that go with the experience can lead to doubts about being able to cope. Unfortunately, the newspapers, magazines, and television commentators can add to these doubts. Many times the paper has us take little "tests" to see if we are depressed, especially around the holidays. It is important to watch for signs of depression, because it is so treatable, and we will cover this in a moment. It is also important to know that many emotions experienced after life events and brain injury are normal. Whatever happened to normal? In the past lots of people viewed their emotions after tragedy—death in the family, loss of businesses, even physical injuries—as normal. It was also considered normal to have intense feelings about these events without making the feeling itself a catastrophe. Somehow people made it through their grieving. Now our newspapers and magazines ask us to take short quizzes to see if we are depressed—because it is a holiday, because we are stay-at-home moms, because we lost a job, or because we have a disabling condition. What about the support for learning how to grieve a loss without being thought odd or sick?

If you or your loved one has experienced a brain injury, we invite you to complete this different sort of questionnaire in Box 4.3.

Most people who are having a normal range of emotions after a brain injury answer "yes" to about 60% or 6 out of 10 of these questions. Loss is a part of the brain injury experience. Rehabilitation doctors have asked clients in their inpatient and outpatient programs the same questions and have found that most report these grief symptoms. While most doctors have found that their clients with brain injury are often not any more depressed than persons without

---

Box 4.3 Normal Reactions to the Normal Losses of Life

Check "Yes" or "No" for Each Item. Since Your Losses:

1. Have you felt anxious about the future? Yes ☐ No ☐

2. Have you noticed you aren't sleeping very well? Yes ☐ No ☐

3. Do you long for the time before your losses? Yes ☐ No ☐

4. Do reminders of what you lost upset you? Yes ☐ No ☐

5. Do you have dreams that you still have what you lost? Yes ☐ No ☐

6. Do you cry or feel like crying when you think about your losses? Yes ☐ No ☐

7. Do you feel the need to talk about your losses? Yes ☐ No ☐

8. Do you think about what you lost so much that it sometimes interferes with what you are trying to do? Yes ☐ No ☐

9. Do you feel angry about your losses? Yes ☐ No ☐

10. Do you feel sad about your losses? Yes ☐ No ☐

disabilities, the feelings the clients are having can be very unpleasant and difficult to deal with. The doctors also know that, on average, 42% of persons with brain injury do develop depression. It is hard for both the doctors and clients to tell the difference between normal grief and sadness and depression, because all the symptoms overlap. Box 4.4 contains a list of normal grief symptoms that have been identified by grief researchers. As you read through the list, think about the losses you have experienced as a result of your brain injury, and note whether you have any of these grief symptoms.

As you read the list in Box 4.4, you will most likely notice how similar grief symptoms are to symptoms of depression and other emotional disorders you may have read about. As with many things in life, a matter of degree is what separates normal from pathological. A person can often tell that they need professional help and may be depressed when certain emotional symptoms are severe and with them most of their waking hours. For example, if a person thinks about their losses so much that they are unable to do daily tasks, unable to sleep for nights at a time, or begin to have thoughts of suicide, they should seek professional help in adjusting to the changes their brain injury has caused. See Box 4.5 for warning signs of depression.

Box 4.4 Normal Grief Symptoms

- Longing for what one has lost

- Feeling like crying or crying about what was lost

- Wishing for the time before the losses

- Sadness about what one lost

- Upset at reminders of what was lost

- Sleep difficulties

- Anxiety about what was lost

Box 4.5 Warning Signs of Depression

1.   You feel depressed almost every day, or someone asks you if you feel depressed.

2.   You have less interest or take little pleasure in almost all of your activities.

3.   You have lost or gained a noticeable amount of weight (such as 5% in one month) or your appetite is much greater or much less than it was before your injury.

4.   You seem to sleep much more or much less than you used to.

5.   You feel agitated or slower almost every day.

6.   You have less energy or feel fatigue almost every day.

7.   You feel worthless or guilty for no reason almost all the time.

8.   You are not able to think or concentrate well or are not able to make decisions, almost every day.

9.   You have repeated thoughts about death (other than fear of dying), you think about suicide often (perhaps have thought of a plan), or have actually made a suicide attempt.

Whether you are the person with the brain injury, or a family member or friend of the person with brain injury, it is important to check with your physician or psychologist to be sure if you have concerns about the possibility of depression. Depression, even after a brain injury, is a very treatable disorder.

Box 4.6 will introduce you to some coping ideas and strategies for common but distressing and uncomfortable grief symptoms and emotions following brain injury. As you look these over, think about which ones would work best for you. Try some out and talk about these with your family members as a way of choosing those that will be most helpful to you. If you are working with a therapist or counselor using this book, they will demonstrate and explain these coping ideas for you.

Box 4.6 Coping with Grief Symptoms and Emotional Reactions Following Brain Injury

Grief Symptom, Behavioral, or Emotional Reaction	How To Manage the Discomfort and Do Damage Control
1. Longing for your old self, too hard on yourself	Reminisce, talk about the past with someone you trust
	Look forward, not backward, to measure your progress
	Don't try to be someone you are not
	Set doable, realistic goals
2. Intrusive thoughts about what you lost or experienced at the time of your injury or illness	Distract yourself with interesting and pleasant activities
	Blink your eyes a lot
3. Have trouble sleeping	Avoid caffeine before bedtime
	Don't take too many naps, don't nap after 3 p.m.
	If severe, ask your doctor for medication
4. Snapping at people you care about	Avoid doing too much at once
	Rest if you need to
	Tell yourself to "Stop and think" before blurting things out
	Use the techniques listed in 7 and 8
5. Worry	Schedule your worry time, only allow yourself to worry then
	Distract yourself with interesting and pleasant activities
6. Fear of what will happen	List or talk about your goals for recovery
	Focus on what you have accomplished so far
	Sit some place that feels safe to you
	Hold onto a familiar and safe object

Box 4.6 Coping with Grief Symptoms and Emotional Reactions Following Brain Injury
Continued

Grief Symptom, Behavioral, or Emotional Reaction	How To Manage the Discomfort and Do Damage Control
7. Difficulty managing stress	▦ Write down each occurrence and train yourself to avoid reacting impulsively by (1) writing down what happened to stress you, (2) what you did, (3) how things turned out, and then (4) what you could do better next time. Rate yourself on how well you managed your stress. Circle a number. 1 — Great! 2 — Pretty Well 3 — Okay 4 — Not so good 5 — Badly At the time of the event, tell yourself encouraging things like "I am stressed, but I think I can stay on top of it." Or "Relax, take a deep breath, let it out slow."
8. Anxiety that disrupts your thoughts	▦ Try the following quick relaxation strategy: Imagine you are on a warm, sandy beach ▦ Close your eyes and let out a long, slow breath ▦ Imagine that you can hear the waves, coming in, going out ▦ Notice your breathing, smooth and even like the sound of the waves ▦ Wave rolls in, you breathe in ▦ Wave rolls out, you exhale ▦ Keep going till you feel calm, sleepy

▓ Brain injury results in losses which bring on normal grief feelings.

▓ Common symptoms of brain injury include difficulties with attention, memory, reasoning, problem solving, restlessness, mood and coping, behavioral control, sleep/wake cycles, swallowing, any of the senses, and muscle weakness and control.

▓ Common symptoms of grief include longing for what was lost, feeling sad about what was lost, wishing for the time before the injury, and being upset by reminders of what was lost.

▓ Everyone grieves in their own way, and length of time it takes varies from person to person. Sometimes people feel a little worse each year on the date of their accident or illness.

▓ People recovering from disabling injuries and illnesses are, in general, only somewhat more likely to be depressed than persons without disabilities. If they do become depressed, and seek the help they need, the disorder is usually treated successfully.

▓ Not only persons with brain injury, but also their families, friends, and others who care for them, may experience a sense of loss.

▓ There are many healthy and productive ways to go through the grieving process and successfully recover emotionally from brain injury.

▓ There are a number of coping strategies that are presented in this book, and that have been helpful for persons adjusting to brain injury, including positive self-talk, keeping active, and planning ahead to prevent depression and fatigue.

In the following Lessons, we will provide you with still more suggestions for coping and emotional recovery plans for both you and your family members. The chapters will provide clear information and ideas to help you navigate through the challenges of brain injury, deal with losses in healthy ways, and move toward strength and renewed interest in living with disability. As with Lesson 4, each of the next Lessons will have exercises and questionnaires with instructions, as well as summary sections to help you remember the main ideas presented. You will learn that actively working to improve your skills or learn compensatory strategies will be restorative and uplifting ways of coping with the normal grief you are experiencing following your brain injury.

Summary

Disabilities resulting from brain injury are like ripples in a pond when you are trying to skip stones. From that one event, the injury, ripples keep moving outward, touching all aspects of a life. The stone hits the water—the injury happens—and the effects spread out over time and relationships. A person can easily feel overwhelmed, sad, confused, afraid, grief-stricken, and defeated. Everyone reacts differently to changes in how they act, look, speak, eat, eliminate, feel, and think. Each person's injury is different. Each person's recovery has a different time frame and course. There are many different ways an injury can affect a person's day-to-day functioning and the people within their social network. You and your friends and family members may experience a range of fluctuating feelings of various intensities throughout the recovery period and beyond. Use of the strategic coping methods and techniques outlined in Lesson 4 will help you overcome these common challenges and move you forward in recovery.

Lesson 5

Anger, Guilt, Acceptance, Denial, and Behavior

Overview

In the preceding Lesson, you learned about patterns of thinking that make coping difficult. In this Lesson, you will begin to learn about specific emotional responses to having a brain injury. There will be two major ideas to learn that will help you feel better and allow you to have control of your own emotions after brain injury. First, you will see (1) where anger and guilt come from, and then (2) apply this information to brain injury. Second, you will discover how to emotionally respond to brain injury effectively.

Goals for This Lesson

■ To learn what makes you feel both angry and guilty

■ To make it easier to reach acceptance

■ To realize the destructive nature of denial

■ To avoid living in the past

Common Responses to Having a Brain Injury

"Why did this happen to me?"

"I can't believe I will ever be happy again."

"Life is over."

"I want to find the person who hit me."

"Leave me alone. I don't want your stupid therapies."

"I feel so guilty that I caused my accident."

"I feel like I am being treated like a child again."

These are common responses and are normal. Most people when faced with as dramatic a change as brain injury will feel overwhelmed and will be flooded with primal emotional reactions. Two primary responses are guilt and anger. While often seen early after the injury, these two emotions can persist for a long time after the injury.

A Common Basis for Anger and Guilt

Although anger and guilt are normal, they can interfere with returning to a satisfying life. You will see that they are very related feelings. They both have their foundation in how you *think* about events. ***Your thoughts are the key to your emotions.*** To understand this, first we will look at events, thoughts, and emotions and then apply that knowledge to anger and guilt.

Tommy as an Example

Suppose Tommy is sitting at his desk late on a Friday and the boss comes in to tell him that he needs to work over the weekend to get a job done. Tommy flashes angry. He remains mad all weekend.

Slowing down that sequence we can see exactly what caused Tommy's anger. Immediately upon hearing what his boss said, Tommy *thought* how unfair the boss's demand was. He wondered why he was being singled out for more work, particularly since he works so hard. He thought that the boss should not make such a request and was not supposed to require weekend work. Tommy's emotions were in response to these thoughts. Unfortunately, these thoughts flashed through his head so quickly he was hardly aware of them. It almost seemed like the event of the boss making the request and the emotion of anger occurred without those thoughts happening. But, they did, and understanding the impact of those thoughts is crucial.

Now imagine the same event but with Tommy thinking different thoughts. Let's consider the impact of these thoughts instead:

"Here is my opportunity to shine. I know there is a promotion coming in my department and I have been looking for a chance to stand out. Maybe my boss selected me because he trusts me and wants to give me this last chance to excel so he can put forth my promotion rather than Joe down the hall."

These thoughts do not trigger anger. Of course, Tommy might still feel disappointed that his weekend plans have to change, but not anger. And the difference? Tommy's thoughts between the event (of his boss's statements) and his emotional response. In fact, in all situations we emotionally react to our ***thoughts*** about an event, ***not*** the event. It is how you view the event and the actions of others that determine your feelings. The good news is that while it is hard to control your feelings, you are in charge of your thoughts and they control your feelings. Unfortunately, most people relate their feelings to events (and the actions of other people) and do not consider their own thoughts; this means they do not decide their own feelings.

How People Usually Relate Events and Feelings

When people experience emotions, they relate the feelings to events. They say things like:

"My wife made me so mad today."

"I am angry that the boss is making me work late again."

"I feel guilty that I did not clean the house today."

The people saying these things are linking their feelings to the events: what the wife did, what the boss did, or what they themselves failed to do. We attribute our feelings to the actions of others or to our own behavior so often that we fail to realize that we do it. Yet, in doing so we miss a crucial component in understanding where feelings come from.

Box 5.1 Events, Thoughts, and Feelings

Events $\longrightarrow$ Thoughts Interpreting $\longrightarrow$ Feelings in Response
the Event to the Interpretation

Dr. Albert Ellis teaches that between events (including our own behavior and the behavior of other people) and feelings are *thoughts*. These thoughts are our interpretation of the event. When an event happens or someone does something, we interpret it (often instantly) *before* we have emotions. This is diagramed in Box 5.1.

This happens so fast we don't even realize that it is happening. If we thought about something differently, we would feel differently about it because our emotions are in response, not to the event, but to our interpretation of the event.

Keep in mind this figure as we explore the thoughts that lead to anger and guilt.

The Emotion of Anger

So, what thoughts do you have when you are angry? Actually, the list is much shorter than most people realize. Whenever you are angry it is always because other people did something you did not think they should do or they failed to do something you thought they should do. Your thoughts will always be one of the following:

"They should (or should not) do …"

"They are supposed to (or not supposed to) do …"

"They have to (or have not to) do …"

"They ought to (or ought not) do …"

"They must (or must not) do …"

Remember, Tommy thought the boss "*should not* make such a request and was *not supposed to* require weekend work."

These words—*should, supposed to, have to, ought to, and must*—set your expectations for other people. The emotion that follows these thoughts is anger. When people do not follow your expectations for them, you get angry with them. Every time you are angry it is because someone else failed to live up to *your* expectations for *them*.

The Emotion of Guilt

If you understand where anger comes from, then it is easy to understand guilt. Guilt is the emotion you feel when you apply the same thoughts to yourself:

"I should (or should not) do …"

"I am supposed to (or not supposed to) do …"

"I have to (or have not to) do …"

"I ought to (or ought not) do …"

"I must (or must not) do …"

And you fail to live up to *your own* expectations.

Again, these words—*should, supposed to, have to, ought to*, and *must*—set your expectations. In this case the expectations you set are for yourself, not for other people. The emotion that follows these thoughts is guilt. When you do not follow your expectations for yourself, you feel guilt. ***Every time*** you feel guilty it is because *you* failed to live up to *your own* expectations.

The thoughts leading to anger and guilt are listed in Box 5.2. Okay, now let's apply our understanding of anger and guilt to brain injury.

Box 5.2 Thoughts Leading to Anger and Guilt

Should	Supposed to	Have to	Ought to	Must

By now you are probably wondering what this has to do with brain injury. Well, after brain injury, it is common to feel anger at other people or guilt over your own actions. Someone else hit you and "He ***should*** have been paying better attention when driving" or "My spouse doesn't understand me after my injury and he ***ought to*** do a better job of it." How about, "My doctor doesn't spend enough time with me and he is ***supposed to*** be more caring."

For guilt, "I ***ought to*** have known to wear a helmet when I went bike riding" or "I was ***supposed to*** be smarter and not drink and drive." Hopefully, you can see the expectation these thoughts convey and the emotions that derive from them.

At this point, before looking at what to do about these thoughts, let us use some examples from your own life.

Exercise

Think about a time when you were angry at another person. Write down what that person did or did not do.

_____

_____

_____

_____

_____

Okay, now write down the "should, supposed to, have to, ought to, or must" thought you applied, even if you did not realize it at the time.

_____

_____

_____

_____

_____

Now do the same thing for an instance when you felt guilty. It is likely to be a different event than the one for anger. What did you do or not do that lead to your guilt?

_____

_____

_____

_____

Finally, what expectations—"should, supposed to, have to, ought to, and must"—for *yourself* did you fail to meet, even if you did not realize it at the time.

_____

_____

_____

_____

What To Do About Thoughts That Lead To Anger and Guilt

There is really good news about these thoughts. You can change them. Most of these expectations for other people and for yourself were learned when you were young from parents, teachers, television, or other kids. You accepted them since you did not know whether or not they were good standards. In fact, as a child you were not allowed to choose your standards: "You will make your bed every day." This was not very negotiable as a little kid. Of course, you were not held very responsible. Nothing really bad happened if you didn't make your bed (although it may have seemed that way at the time).

As a teenager, you began to have some freedom to set your own standards: "You should be home by 10 p.m." "Can't I stay out until 10:30 p.m.?" "Okay, but you had better show you can handle it and be on time or you will be grounded forever." You had some say and the penalties went up. Another example with more significant consequences might have been, "All right don't study, but you won't get into college." When you were a teenager you began to understand the link between choices and real-world responsibilities.

As an adult you get to decide what standards you want, but you are wholly responsible for the consequences. Still, you are not required to live by standards chosen for you by other people. If you don't want to make your bed, it is okay, as long as you don't mind the mess. If you choose to pay your bills late, it is okay, as long as you don't mind affecting your credit rating. If you do not work hard, you will probably not get promoted or get a raise. You choose and you are responsible.

Box 5.3 summarizes the relationship between freedom to choose and responsibility.

Choosing Your Thoughts

The problem is most adults don't choose. They continue to live according to the expectations they learned a long time ago. What you believe is proper is often what you learned as a child, but now those standards may be interfering with your happiness after brain injury. See how this works with some examples below.

"Good people work" translates as "I am *supposed to* be employed," implying that you are a failure if you are not working. *But* you really know you lost your job because of your injury, not because you don't want to work. "Achieve independence" translates as "I *should not* need help with mobility, managing my finances, and making

---

Box 5.3 Freedom to Choose and Responsibility

Stage of life	Freedom to Choose	Responsibility
Child	Very little	Very little
Teenager	Increasing	Increasing
Adult	Total	Complete

decisions," implying that you are less worthwhile if you need help. *But* you really know that people with medical conditions sometimes do need assistance. "Pay attention and be reliable" translates as "To show people I am competent, I ***ought to*** attend to details and complete tasks on time," implying that you are useless if you do not manage your time and cognitively process well. *But* you really know that your medical condition causes these, just as someone who loses a leg has trouble walking. See Box 5.4.

These examples demonstrate how easy it is to feel worthless and useless if you base your emotions on thoughts learned a long time ago. Instead, as an adult you can change how you view events by changing the thoughts that dictate your emotions. Look at the following examples.

So let's change the thinking in this example to: "I'd prefer to work, but I can still feel good about myself if I don't work. I can do other things such as being a peer counselor, volunteering, serving on a government committee on brain injury, helping to lobby my legislature on laws about brain injury, serving on a hospital citizens' committee, etc." Another positive thought might be: "I am contributing to society by spending more time with my kids." See Box 5.5.

Examples of Changed Thoughts

Hopefully, you can see how rethinking things changes how you feel. Guilt is replaced by hope, satisfaction, or pride in this example.

Here are other challenges about which you could feel angry or guilty, but as shown below can be thought about differently.

Box 5.4 Example of Thoughts Leading to Guilt

Event		Thought/Interpretation		Emotion
Not working	⟶	"I am supposed to work. I am a failure if I am not working."	⟶	Guilt

---

Box 5.5 Thoughts Leading to Positive Emotions

Event   ⟶   Thought/Interpretation   ⟶   Emotion

Not working   ⟶   "I'd like to work, but there are   ⟶   Hope,
other things that are also important   Satisfaction,
in life. I can be productive and   Pride
useful in lots of ways. My self-worth
is not tied to working. I am free
to do other great things."

"Yes, I need help with mobility, managing my finances, and making decisions, but I use that as an opportunity. I can teach others about how to help people with needs similar to my own. This can be a two-way street with my getting the help I need in exchange for teaching my providers the best way to help people."

"I am not good at details and time management now. Instead I will look for opportunities to help people see the big picture. Too many people get lost in the daily grind of details to have long-term vision. Plus, working on thinking about the big picture often is less time dependent than solving the immediate crisis."

Exercise

In the previous exercise you wrote down an example of a situation in which you became angry and one in which you were guilty. Now take the "angry" example and write down how you could rethink your thoughts about the situation in a manner that does not include "should, ought to, supposed to, have to, or must." Essentially, you are being asked to judge the behavior of the other person or the event differently!

_____

_____

_____

_____

_____

If you *think* about it in this new way, do you feel differently? Do you feel differently than angry? You may still not approve of the situation or person. You may feel disappointed or hurt. But, without "should, ought to, supposed to, have to, or must," you cannot produce anger.

Okay, now do the same thing for the example you had when you felt guilty. Write down a different way to think about it ...

_____

_____

_____

_____

_____

... and eliminate the guilt. You still may wish you had done something differently. You still may feel dissatisfied with yourself, but you do not feel guilty.

Why Remove Anger and Guilt

Questioning why to remove guilt and anger may seem odd since there is little reason to think that anyone would want to feel either emotion. After all, what is so much better about disappointment compared to anger or dissatisfaction compared to guilt? The answer is that guilt and anger are so destructive to you. Decreasing anger and guilt is healthy. Guilt and anger increase your stress; however, disappointment, dissatisfaction, or other emotions let you make more reasoned judgments and create in you the freedom to problem solve, learn from experience, and to forgive yourself or others.

Next Steps Next Time

Reframing your thoughts in the manner shown changes your emotions. Your emotions are no longer a function of old standards and expectations. So, there are a few steps to make it easier.

- Every time you think a thought using "should, supposed to, have to, ought to, or must," write down the thought.

- Think about where you learned that standard for your own behavior or the behavior of someone else. Who taught you that thought?

- Upon reflection now as an adult, do you think that it is a good, healthy, reasonable thought, standard, or expectation for you? Is it making you happier, more content, less angry, or less guilty?

- If it is harmful to you, now is the time to change it. You can choose; you do not have to live your life by outdated thoughts that no longer apply to you.

By the way, it is often also interesting to write down every time someone else tells you that you "should, supposed to, have to, ought to, or must" do something, or not do something. All day long people will lay their expectations on you. You will probably be amazed at how often other people want you to act as they want you to and will hope you will feel guilty if you have different expectations for yourself once you write them down on the form.

Box 5.6 can be copied and used as a log of your anger- or guilt-producing thoughts (arising from you or other people) and the alternative thoughts that make you feel better.

Acceptance

If you can let go of your old thoughts you are now ready to consider acceptance of your injury. Again, this is easier to say than to do, but it is within your grasp. Here is what trips up most people. Most people believe acceptance involves no longer letting the injury upset them. When someone says to you that, "You have to accept the injury and get on with your life," it implies they believe that you should no longer worry about it or be bothered by it.

That is unrealistic. It can even be irritating when people imply that you quit worrying about it. You may find yourself wanting to verbally lash out at them about their seemingly simple attitude about the struggles you may be having. At best, they appear to misunderstand brain injury and, at worst, are dismissive of the challenges you face and the changes to your life. If you believe, like they might believe, that acceptance means, "be fine with your injury," you will find it very hard to achieve acceptance.

Box 5.6 Log of Anger- and Guilt-Producing Thoughts

For Anger

Date	Event/ Behavior of other person	Your thought: They should, ought to, supposed to, have to must .... (or should not ...)	Your new thought

For Guilt

Date	Your behavior	Your thought: I should, ought to, supposed to, have to, Must ... (or should not ...) or What someone else told you you should ...	Your new thought

Fortunately, there is another kind of acceptance that is achievable. In fact, most people who are successful in their emotional outlook after injury achieve this type of acceptance. This type of acceptance sounds like this: "I hate my injury. If I had one wish it would be to wish it away. **But**, it is not going away because I don't like it. So, I can have strong negative emotions about the injury and still do the best I can. I do not have to be happy about the injury to no longer dwell on it."

The challenge is to be able to hold in your mind and heart two separate ideas: "This is bad; I can have a good life anyway and be at peace." The hard part is holding onto two seemingly conflicting ideas: "I don't like this" and "It isn't going to stop me." Note, however, that nowhere in those two thoughts is "It doesn't bother me." Rather, you do not have to be frozen in place by your dislike of the brain injury.

To achieve this acceptance, you can still regret the injury. You can even be mad about it, if you choose. You can miss the life you had before the injury. **But**, the injury is not all there is to know about you and it is not your total life. You can achieve, love, fail, succeed, hope, etc., even with the injury. Life awaits you.

Exercise

It is worth taking a moment to write down the thoughts (and feelings) that have stopped you from achieving acceptance. These are the ones that seem to conflict with acceptance. Perhaps the thoughts are, "I can never be the same as I was" or "This is unfair." Whatever they are, write them down here.

Thoughts That Seem To Conflict with Acceptance

_____

_____

_____

_____

_____

Now, the crucial step is to realize that you can still have those thoughts, if you want, but get on with your life. There is nothing about those thoughts that has to stop you from participating in the best life you can build. How do you do that?

When you stop viewing yourself as a "brain-injured person," and stop thinking, "I am brain injured," and begin to think of yourself as a "person with a brain injury," you change your focus from the injury being all someone would need to know about you. When you change your view to the brain injury being one thing about you as person, along with lots of other things, some of which you like and some of which you do not like, you open up possibilities for your life. When you accept your brain injury in this manner, it becomes something to deal with, not something to freeze you in place. You don't have to like your injury to be happy with your life.

People who achieve acceptance after brain injury view their injuries as an important part of them, but it is not the only part of them. They find acceptance through looking at their whole self. The brain injury does not remove your capacity to have accomplishments, relationships, disappointments, dreams, etc.

Acceptance is difficult if you view your injury as all encompassing. Acceptance is achievable, if you view your injury as part of you, but only a part.

The most crucial message is:

> **THE BRAIN INJURY IS ONLY A PART OF YOU.**
> **YOU ARE A *PERSON* WITH A BRAIN INJURY,**
> **NOT A BRAIN-INJURED PERSON!**

Identity and Acceptance

You are valuable and important. Brain injury does not change that. The challenge is to get used to asserting that fact and not view yourself as dependent, with little to contribute to society.

Moreover, independence is a myth. We tell ourselves that we are independent so that we can feel secure. It comforts us because it makes us feel better to think that we could survive alone. After brain injury you learn that you need other people, but so does everyone else. In this awareness you are smarter than other people. You know that you need other people, and that they need you: you are ahead of the game. You can work on relationships and your participation in society purposefully. True independence comes not from being able to act alone, but from being so well enmeshed with other people that you are both valued and safe, and simultaneously value and help others.

Moreover, the issues you must address are often based in society's limited view. Dr. Rhoda Olkin writes that having a disability makes you part of a minority group. It is the only disability group you join. You join through brain injury, spinal cord injury, polio, diabetes, etc. It is the largest minority group in the country. If you conceptualize yourself now as part of a minority group, your approach to life can change. Minority groups add strength to society.

To understand this, let's step back from brain injury for a moment and look at four examples.

Case Examples

Imagine all of the trees in a forest are the same kind (e.g., elm trees). An insect attacks the forest and likes elm trees in particular, destroying all of them. It wipes out the forest. Instead, if some trees were elms and some were oaks and some were pine trees, the forest would survive. Diversity is crucial.

Consider a football team that has too many wide receivers and linemen but only two running backs. When both get hurt there is no one to fill in and the team does poorly having to rely on throwing the ball too much. The team suffers because it lacked diversity. In football, you need linemen, safeties, quarterbacks, and running backs, all with different skills.

Think about a so-called individual sport like tennis. If the tennis player had to truly operate alone, the player would do poorly. Why? Because the player needs coaches, agents, and trainers with different knowledge and skills. There is no such thing as an individual alone in sport, though we like to pretend there is.

Finally look at work. The best performing workplaces have people with different perspectives. Most of us have been with people who came up with an idea we would not have thought of because of their unique life experiences, training, etc. When companies become too narrow in their thinking (group think), they fail to see market threats and get left behind when things change. Diversity protects us; so called independence does not.

Being like everyone else is not a strength. You have a unique contribution to make to any group you join. Your experiences add diversity, and it is that richness that is valuable to help others. Just like any minority group member, you can act like your minority membership is an asset or a limitation.

Exercise

Based upon the preceding reading try to imagine what your unique contributions might be to a group you belong to or would like to join. What life experiences have you had that might benefit the group? What knowledge have you gained? What life lessons can you contribute? Writing those down below will help you begin to see the strengths you have.

My Potential Contributions Based on My Life Experiences

_____

_____

_____

_____

It is also important to realize that your "limits" are more likely a reflection of society than they are of you. Dr. Al Condeluci teaches that we are all "interdependent." The idea is that when people encounter limitations, they attribute these to themselves rather than to how society functions. This is a mistake.

Tammy as an Example

Tammy cannot walk and is in a wheelchair. She cannot get into an inaccessible building. She feels it is her problem for not being able to walk. People have said to her she cannot do office work because she lacks the skill to walk around the inaccessible space.

Is the problem one of walking (and therefore her problem) or one of building design (and therefore the employer's problem who loses a great worker)? It depends on how we define the "disability." Maybe the problem is a "disabled building" that does not facilitate access! Maybe instead of saying she has a disability we should say the employer has a dysfunctional building and that she is perfectly fine?

After brain injury, interdependence argues that if we value your contribution, as we should, then all of us should provide support for that contribution and identify the barriers (cognitive, emotional, behavioral, physical, etc.) that interfere.

Denial

Acceptance does not mean denying problems. You still must know the issues you have to deal with to move forward. There are two kinds of denial after brain injury:

- Psychological denial

- Organic denial

Psychological Denial

The first type, psychological denial, is actually common to most people. It can occur in regard to brain injury or anything else that is hard to face. ***Psychological denial occurs when something is too painful to admit as being true about yourself.*** It represents something that you find so painful to acknowledge that you reject its validity. If you have psychological denial about your injury, or its fallout, then it is likely that the injury has effected your core beliefs about who you are and how you value yourself. This is frequently true after brain injury and is normal. After all, you have been through a dramatic shift in your abilities and may feel your self-concept has been under attack.

In such situations it is common to see a self-protective response involving psychological denial. If you can ignore some of the problems you are having, then it will be easier to hang on to your core beliefs—financial stability, independence, good looks, athletic prowess, intelligence, etc.,—about who you are. Still, with psychological denial you know what the truth is, it just hurts to admit it.

Case Example of Psychological Denial

Tommy wants to get back to work. He insists he is ready to his health care workers. When his wife expresses concerns about his balance, he gets angry at her. He even tries to walk close to walls or stay at the back of a group of friends when walking so they cannot see if he stumbles. He purposefully leaves his cane at home when he goes out.

However, in his heart he knows he is less steady than before his injury. He is very fearful of not being able to go back to his own job. When he insists that he can do so, he hopes everyone believes him. He is really seeking someone who will validate his statements that he can work so that he can feel reassured. He is terrified of the consequences of not working and that people will think less of him. However, he is very concerned that balance problems will get in the way of his job.

Tommy knows he has a balance issue. It is just so scary to admit it because it has large implications for him about who he is as a breadwinner and a man. He is doing everything he can to avoid the truth he knows. This is psychological denial.

Can you think of a time when you knew something to be so, but it was too painful to admit? Did you avoid thinking about what you knew to be true? Did you tell yourself things that would disprove what you suspected was true, so that you felt better? Maybe you are still telling yourself these things and have not yet been honest with yourself. Confronting the truth can be painful; you can no longer hide behind the story you have told yourself. Still, if you are honest with yourself, you will be more effective in life. It is impossible to be your best when your actions are based on falsehoods you generate to protect yourself from reality.

Exercise

Try writing down one idea you have made up about yourself since your injury that you know in your heart is not true.

_____

_____

_____

_____

If you told yourself the truth what would it be? Write that down, too.

_____

_____

_____

_____

Now consider how you would act, what would you say, how would you think if you based it honestly upon the truth. How would you be more effective? Do other people know the truth and don't tell you because they do not want to hurt you? Are they afraid of offending you? Would you be closer to these people if both of you were honest? Would you get more support?

_____

_____

_____

_____

Perhaps it is time to drop the stories you tell yourself (and others) and be the person you really are?

Organic Denial

The other type of denial after brain injury, called organic denial (in fancy health care terms, the word you may hear is _anosognosia_), is different and is only seen among people who have had brain injury.

In organic denial you are unaware of the problems, in contrast to psychological denial where you are aware but do not confront the problems. Because the brain is injured and it is the examining tool, when it looks at itself to see how it is doing, it adds up the data wrong and concludes it is fine.

Case Example of Organic Denial

Jeannie believes her memory is fine after her injury. Other people have pointed out to her that she forgets things a lot now but she does not believe them. In fact, she got very upset with a friend the last time this happened. Her friend mentioned to her that she missed their lunch date in spite of his having called the day before to remind her, but she denied that he had called. She accused him of lying to make himself look good and to make her look foolish. She said to him that maybe he was making up his so-called reminder call so that he could blame her for not coming and drop her as a friend.

If one has memory problems, the brain forgets when it forgot something; it thinks it is doing fine. When your brain tells you something entirely different from what everyone else tells you, and then you ***refuse to even consider*** that maybe they know something you don't, you are experiencing organic denial.

This only happens after brain injury. If you did not have a brain injury, but, for example, had a broken leg, your brain would correctly see the facts—inability to walk, leg pain, bone sticking out through the skin, lots of blood—and correctly conclude: "my leg is broken." In contrast, when the brain is injured, it examines ***itself*** after brain injury, it adds up all the "known" facts, and it gives you the wrong answer!

Organic denial is very hard for people to address because the brain insists it is right. Can you recall a time since your injury when other people, who you normally would have trusted, gave you feedback or disagreed with you and you fought with them, ignored them, or insisted that they were wrong? Did you consider the information they had? Were you 100% certain they were wrong? Were you willing to explore their idea?

Exercise

Okay, let's take a look at a time when other people gave you feedback and you continued to pursue a course of action. What was it that you wanted to do?

_____

_____

_____

_____

_____

What feedback did you get from other people?

_____

_____

_____

_____

_____

If these people were people you listened to in the past before your injury, what were the reasons you told yourself to ignore them now? If they were professionals (e.g., psychologist, physician, case manager), what reasons did you have for discounting their experience?

_____

_____

_____

_____

Maybe it is time to consider that when you receive similar input from multiple people that there is truth to the feedback? Of course, there may be times when you want to swim against the tide; despite the belief of others, you may want to pursue a course of action. Still, you must consider, if you are wrong what harm do you incur? How risky is the path you want to follow? Sometimes there is little harm, and it is safe to try something, and sometimes there is great financial or bodily harm that can occur if you ignore other people's advice.

Why Addressing Denial is Crucial for Acceptance

Acceptance includes dealing with both psychological denial and organic denial. If you want to succeed, you cannot ignore your injury. If you have cognitive processing problems, for example, and you deny (either type of denial) their existence, you will have difficulty being successful. The rest of the world will see the errors you make and will take into consideration your real abilities on a given task, not the abilities you want to have (psychological denial) or the skills you think you have (organic denial). The real world judges on performance. To accept your injury means being honest with yourself. Denial gets in the way of that. It is very difficult to achieve anything in life if you do not know your own strengths and weaknesses.

Psychological Denial and Acceptance

When you address psychological denial by examination of your beliefs about how you were supposed to live, you change your expectations for yourself. If you can be comfortable with different standards then you can begin to feel less defensiveness about the abilities you have lost. Psychological denial only occurs when you need to live up to a standard. It is better to choose to change the standard than live, unsuccessfully, in denial.

Organic Denial and Acceptance

Organic denial is trickier, because at its core you don't realize the truth. Your brain is giving you false information. That can be hard to recognize. One person with brain injury once went 17 years insisting that he could do his old job and refused to accept other work, despite feedback from family, friends, professionals, and most importantly his former employer, that he no longer had the skills for his old job, but that there were lots of other things for which he did have the skills. He refused for 17 years after his brain injury to work at anything else. Wow. It is important to listen to the feedback you get from other people. It is unwise to ignore an accumulation of evidence over time.

Despite its crucial importance, awareness that underlies acceptance can be hard. As your awareness improves you may actually feel worse. During denial you may feel better than when you confront your injury. In fact, psychologists in rehabilitation centers commonly hear people saying that "as I get better, I feel worse." You may experience increasing distress as you become more insightful about the challenges you face. In some ways you may feel that "ignorance is bliss," and as awareness increases you are angrier and more depressed. Plus, you may gain awareness of your situation before you have the emotional coping skills to deal with your sense of loss. Be assured that this is normal and working your way through this book can help.

A final Trap To Avoid

Acceptance is hard to achieve if you compare your life before and after your injury.

A Case Example

Imagine Linda is walking on a trail. She reaches a fork in the road. She will have different experiences in life down one path versus the other path. She may meet someone on one path and not the other. Perhaps she falls in love with that person. However, she also trips badly breaking her leg. Down the other route she might find a lost and injured dog that she rescues. The owner is wealthy and donates a large sum of money to her favorite cause, but she is so distressed over the dog's injuries that she develops trouble sleeping.

Who knows? In each moment of life things happen that take your life one way or the other. We have all heard of someone who misses an airplane flight that crashes. Consider even smaller events. You get up a little late in the morning and just miss being in the line at the coffee shop and so never meet someone who would have been a wonderful influence in your life. You will never know what wonderful and troublesome things await you on every path. It is impossible to compare the life you have with the life you missed, because you don't know what would have happened down the road at each choice point.

If you contrast your current problems with your imagined successes on the other road, you will find that it is impossible to achieve acceptance and you will probably be depressed. There were certainly bad things also likely to happen to you, along with the good, on the other path, but it is hard to conceive of what tragedies (e.g., death of a child, getting a disease, loss of a job, divorce, etc.) might have happened. It is also impossible for you to know yet what tremendous success, great influences, or soaring achievements you will have in your life with brain injury.

Look at Figure 5.1. It shows the losing game that many people with brain injury play when they compare their current struggles with their imagined lost future successes. They ignore unknown disasters on their old life course, as well as the good things on their current path.

Let's see how you think about Figure 5.1 in the following exercise.

Exercise

Try writing down the achievements and successes you foresaw in your life before your injury.

_____

_____

_____

_____

_____

Now make a list of your current challenges.

_____

_____

_____

_____

_____

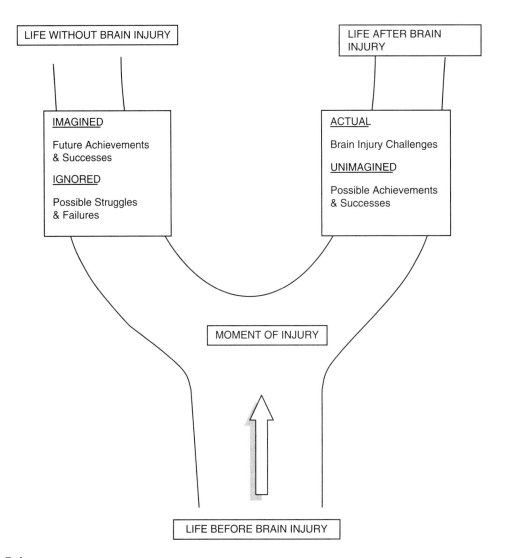

Figure 5.1

Comparison of life paths

Okay, that was the easy part. So, finally imagine possible future achievements and successes you might reach in life now.

_____

_____

_____

_____

_____

When you can write down this last part easily, you are on your way to changing how you view yourself and your potential.

If it is hard to imagine successes, do not be frustrated. Some of the best things may not even be known to you during your life. Teachers, for example, shape lives in ways they may never know about: an elementary school teacher who helps a struggling student learn to read and 25 years later the student becomes a doctor. That teacher will never know, but had there been a different, less invested teacher, the student might have never learned to read well and so would have quit high school at some point.

The only way to even have a chance of knowing what you will accomplish is to live your current life to the best of your abilities and see what happens. You must embrace life, even with the brain injury, if you want to enhance the likelihood of having good things happen. If you are angry or guilty you will be frozen. So, don't burden yourself with the impossible comparison of lost greatness and current hurdles, ignoring unknown missed disasters and your current potential for wonderful things.

Reaching Acceptance

It is impossible for there to be a comprehensive list of all the ways that interfere with getting on with life. Still, a few thoughts are common to many people and can serve as examples for how to proceed. Consider whether the following thoughts sound familiar to you: "The injury is unfair. No one should have to put up with the fallout of a brain injury. Such things are not supposed to happen to people. One's life ought not to include such harmful injuries. I was supposed to be able to live a more normal life. I have to raise a family; I must earn a living."

Look again at the last six sentences. Every one of those sentences includes a "should, supposed to, have to, ought to, or must." Yet, we know that there are estimated to be 1.5 million traumatic brain injuries every year and about 700,000 people suffer a stroke annually.

So, despite the overwhelming evidence that lots of people get hurt, we all think that we are "supposed to be" immune.

Can you see the sequence from event to thought to emotion to nonacceptance? You have a brain injury (event). "I am not supposed to have a brain injury" (thought). "I am angry" (emotion). "I can't believe that this happened to me"(nonacceptance).

Instead, try this on for fit. "I have a brain injury" (event). "Life is risky and lots of people get hurt. I participated fully in life, driving places, playing sports, doing home repair on a ladder, etc., and there was a chance I might get hurt. Plus, I know that my value in life is based on the type of person I am, loving, kind, helpful, etc., not how much money I earn or how good I look, etc., so I know that I can be a great person even with my injury" (thought). "I am not happy with my injury, but I am participating in life to the best of my abilities" (acceptance).

This feels different because of the thoughts. Now obviously those thoughts do not have to be your thoughts. You can think whatever you want. If you choose your thoughts in such a way as to not lead to anger or guilt, you create room for acceptance.

Behavioral Symptoms of Nonacceptance

Acceptance is hard. It takes a daily effort to keep focused on moving forward and not looking back. Yet, you may find yourself frustrated with the struggle. This is normal. In trying to adapt to your new circumstances you may experience strong emotions. Sometimes people after brain injury have difficulty expressing their feelings directly and this may happen to you.

Expressing feelings can be hard because one must acknowledge having the feeling, overcome hesitancy to disclose the emotion to other people, have the language skills to communicate the feeling, and remember the words to describe emotions. For some people after brain injury the barriers to addressing their feelings are so high that the feelings are expressed only indirectly through their behavior.

Are you expressing your emotions through your behavior? Do you act in self-destructive ways because of guilt, anger, grief, etc? Do other people misunderstand your behavior? They may attribute it to the wrong emotion—one you are not having. They may not provide you with the help you would like. The problem is that indirect expression of emotion through behavior leads to miscommunication. If you use behaviors such as withdrawal, noncompliance, demanding things of other people, etc., you risk being misunderstood by other people.

Exercise

If you can, write down a time when you acted based on your feelings which you did not discuss and ended up being misunderstood.

_____

_____

_____

_____

_____

What emotions were you struggling to discuss?

_____

_____

_____

_____

_____

Were there negative consequences to not relating your feelings more directly?

_____

_____

_____

_____

_____

What could you have said instead of acting out your feelings indirectly?

_____

_____

_____

One problem with not discussing your emotions is that your message may not get through to other people. You might do better with a more direct approach. A second problem with indirectly communicating your emotions through behavior is that other people may decide to step in and take control away from you, if your behavior is dangerous to other people (e.g., hitting, throwing things, or threatening other people), or if your behavior is dangerous to yourself (e.g., running away, trying suicide, using poor judgment that places you at risk for harm). If your behavior is inappropriate, such as hoarding things, stealing, being sexually inappropriate, being socially inappropriate, then they will once more curtail your independence.

When your frustration spills over into behavioral acting out in a way that puts you or others at risk, you are in trouble, and it would be best to seek professional help.

Summary

Achievable acceptance will not remove your sense of grief or loss, nor should it. Grief is part of acceptance. Recall that part of achievable acceptance is acknowledging that your brain injury is real. You have gone through a significant event. Accepting its reality while proceeding with your life still means that it is all right to admit to a sense of loss due to the injury. The goal, after all, is not to deny the changes, but to avoid getting frozen in place by them. If you can change the anger and guilt that may freeze you in place, and address your denial, then acceptance comes easier. Grief, however, is part of acceptance.

Lesson 6

Coping—How To Maintain a Healthy Outlook

Overview

The purpose of Lesson 6 is to give persons with brain injury the tools and knowledge they need to identify and avoid or counteract several self-defeating thinking and attitude pitfalls. You may have noticed your losses related to your brain injury and are possibly having a range of sad and angry feelings about these losses. These feelings are usually part of normal grieving. Unfortunately, the feelings can be so intense and unpleasant that people begin to turn on themselves through harsh self-talk and self-judgments. Lesson 6 will provide you with specific suggestions for dealing with grief without resorting to self-abuse, and with consistent and practiced use of proactive coping strategies.

Goals for This Lesson

- Learn how to self-assess thoughts, judgments, and feelings about yourself and your situation

- Learn about 5 self-defeating thought habits and how to conquer them to improve your recovery

- Learn how to use a process of goal-attainment scaling

- Learn ways to prevent hopelessness and despair

How About You?

The early days of recovery after brain injury are often a blur to clients in the hospital. Think back to the early days of recovery. Can you recall experiencing common injury problems like disturbed sleep-wake cycles, drowsiness, distractibility, or an altered sense of time? If you are not able to remember, has someone in your family or a friend ever told you about your early behavior and symptoms? When did you begin to realize that you had gone through a significant, life-changing event? When did you start to notice changes in yourself? Did it take you longer to get dressed? Were you having trouble remembering therapists' names and instructions? Could you read your own handwriting? While even remembering these early insights into changes can be alarming and upsetting, and it was probably alarming back then as well, remembering will help you get the most out of this Lesson.

Self-Defeating Thinking Patterns

Rehabilitation providers working with persons following brain injury report that their clients make comments like those in Box 6.1 all too often.

These kinds of thoughts may remind you of some of the feelings discussed in the first two Lessons. Most likely these comments were made by people who were feeling afraid, upset, and maybe even negative or hopeless. As was discussed in Lesson 4, people with brain injury sometimes reach a point where they compare their abilities after injury with those they remember having prior to injury. The comparison is not logical, because the person was not challenged before the brain injury like they are after the injury. However, many people fall into this trap after a brain injury. As we discussed in

---

Box 6.1 Self-Defeating Thoughts After Brain Injury

"I used to be able to dress for work and be on my way in 10 minutes, now I need help to stand and pull up my pants!"

"My memory is shot! I can't remember anything!"

"I am just here with my brains scrambled! I can't do anything productive anymore."

"Why should I even try, I can't do anything right?"

Lesson 4, people with brain injury often make these kinds of illogical comparisons and add to their difficulties because they might begin to dislike themselves or feel despair. As a result, the very people around them that they rely on for support might pull away because they are uncomfortable about the survivor's negativity and grouchiness. Let's look at Dale's story.

Dale as Wounded Warrior

Dale was fortunate to survive seven months in Iraq. He was pretty lucky. While he got involved in some fire fights, he endured them all without injury. There were a couple of times on patrol when a bomb exploded, twice throwing him on the ground. However, he was happy to find that he could just get up, brush himself off, and keep going. After the second blast he noticed a few changes. He was grouchy and his sergeant reported that Dale was forgetting to follow through on tasks. Dale was referred to the base hospital for evaluation when these symptoms got worse, and he started arguing with other soldiers to the point of causing fist fights. After a brief examination, he was transferred to the major Army hospital in Langstuhl, Germany for an evaluation to rule out a brain injury. By this time Dale started to see that he was having trouble with memory. Even simple day-to-day tasks seemed overwhelming. Then there were the headaches. Diagnostic testing did reveal that the blasts Dale had been exposed to during combat episodes resulted in two small bleeds within his brain. The neurologist did not think surgery was necessary, as these were healing, but the rehabilitation team recommended Dale have rehabilitation. Then there was the post-traumatic stress disorder (PTSD) that resulted in Dale seeing some horrible scenes from combat over and over again. He was having bad dreams and trouble sleeping. Dale's wife and children were able to join him in Germany. He was so happy to see them, but was embarrassed to have them see him unable to remember events and things said to him on a day-to-day basis. He began to tell himself he was worthless, damaged beyond repair. His wife and parents tried to encourage him but he snapped at them and often refused to make an effort during his rehabilitation therapies. After three weeks he began making very slow progress and could finally be persuaded to really work in therapies. He met a psychologist at the veteran's hospital who helped him begin talking through his terrible memories of his war experiences. At first, it was hard to talk about these memories. After awhile he looked forward to having this place to talk openly about his feelings and concerns. Dale's wife was supporting and encouraging him, but he remained irritable and unsympathetic to her issues. She did have their two children to take care of and felt really alone with this. His in-laws moved closer to help the family. Dale got an honorable discharge from the Army, but was not able to get a civilian job. Most days he watched television in his bedroom. He was able to continue his therapies at a local Veteran's Administration hospital. Dale told himself that he was useless and there was no point in trying to look for work or work on his relationship with his wife. Unfortunately, his marriage did not last.

As it turns out, though dealing with brain injury was very challenging, some of Dale's adjustment problems may have been related to his inner thoughts and self-defeating behaviors. In Lesson 4 we talked about how important it is to avoid the trap of comparing abilities from before the brain injury to those after. We talked about the importance of self-acceptance of brain injury deficits. Dale was challenged by being a veteran of Iraq, by having a brain injury, and by having PTSD. He did not do himself a favor by also telling himself that he was worthless and damaged beyond repair. The outlook and coping style that people with brain injury use, both in the beginning and during ongoing recovery, affect motivation, the amount of energy put toward rehabilitation, the emotions and emotional health of family, and how well they recover. Unfortunately, negative outlooks are not always obvious or easy to identify, especially by the person with the brain injury. The person with the brain injury, because of their common thinking and problem-solving difficulties, may need help to get out of the pit.

To get ready for learning a new set of strategies, look over and fill out the "Attitude Makeover Questionnaire" in Box 6.2. The new strategies you will learn will help you counteract tendencies to think about the worst possible outcomes and aspects of your situation. An important first step in learning to manage strong worries and feelings, and thus improve your outlook, is to really understand how you think and feel about your situation. Take the survey in Box 6.2 to learn about how you are seeing yourself and your situation.

Box 6.2 *Attitude Makeover Questionnaire*
              Check *All Statements* You Say To Yourself:

1. *I try to look on the bright side of every situation.* ☐

2. **I let my whole family down.** ☐

3. **Why am I so stupid? I can't remember anything!** ☐

4. *I think I am making good progress in my recovery.* ☐

5. **If I can't do everything just like I did before my injury, it will be terrible!** ☐

6. *I am really thankful for my therapists, family, and friends who are encouraging me and helping me get better.* ☐

7. **I don't plan on going back to work unless I can get the same job I had before my accident.** ☐

8. **Other people I know at my rehabilitation center are walking and able to work in about three weeks after rehab. I am still here after two months! What's wrong with me?** ☐

9. *I am having a tough time but I believe, with work, I can get better.* ☐

You may have noticed that some statements on the questionnaire are in boldface. The boldface means that these are negative comments. However, even if you checked mostly bolded statements, or wrote some negative comments about your current skills, some of the coping ideas covered in Lesson 4 may help you change to a more positive outlook. You may find out that you are a primary cause of your own misery. If that is true, changing what you say to yourself will be a key to feeling better. If you checked mostly italicized items, and evaluated yourself well in your written comments, you most likely have a positive outlook. Now and in your future recovery, focusing more on how things could go well instead of how they could turn out badly, will help you become better able to face any continuing challenges. Whether you checked either boldface or italic items, or a mixture, you will likely find the next pages helpful for learning how to be more nurturing and kind to yourself as you heal from your injury. You will be learning some strategies to help improve your attitude toward yourself and recovery.

Now complete the exercise in Box 6.3. Ask someone you trust to help you if writing is difficult for you now. The "What Are You Saying to Yourself?" exercise will help you identify whether you are making negative comments to yourself and risking harm to your confidence and recovery.

Now we will go over five specific thinking habits and pitfalls that can worsen your self-view, dampen your hopes for the future, and interfere with your progress. As you work through these pitfalls, look back at your responses to the "What Are You Saying to Yourself?" questionnaire you just completed in Box 6.3. Based on the responses you wrote down, are you using self-defeating thinking?

Look at Box 6.4 to read about the first of five "Outlook Pitfalls." We will describe and tell you how to avoid these nasty habits of thinking.

Box 6.3 What Are You Saying to Yourself?
Use the Lines Below To Record How You Talk To Yourself About Your:

Memory _____

_____

Thinking _____

_____

Speech _____

_____

Abilities _____

_____

Strengths _____

_____

Progress in Recovery _____

_____

Now read over the examples and complete the form in Exercises A and B in Boxes 6.5 and 6.6. See if you are saying these kinds of things to yourself.

Consider Joe's Approach

Joe was thinking about returning to work. His brain injury rehabilitation outpatient therapists and vocational counselors were encouraging him to begin applying for food service jobs. Prior to injury Joe

Box 6.6 Exercise B: Positive Comparisons — My Early and Later Recovery Days

What I Am Able To Do Today?	What I Could Do the Day After My Injury?

had been a junior manager for a fast food restaurant. Joe told his counselors "before I was injured, I supervised a staff of six employees. I don't want to make hamburgers in the back. I am not able to walk straight yet, and I still feel too tired. I will wait until I improve and then apply for my old job." Joe had a severe brain injury when a deer hit his company car. He had made excellent progress since his injury, but continued to have memory, balance, and vision problems. His counselors were recommending that, because of his great progress, his current strengths could result in a good, solid full-time or part-time job at this entry level. However, rather than take the work, and the increased independence and confidence it might bring him, Joe's comparison with his past self did not allow him to see how much progress it took to get to his current status. He missed an opportunity because he was stuck in a negative comparison with the past.

Look at Box 6.7 to read about the second of the five "Outlook Pitfalls" to self-assess and avoid.

The second self-defeating comparison is between *you and someone else with a brain injury.* No two brain injuries, recovery rates, or symptom lists are the same. While it may be natural and tempting to compare yourself with others who seem to be doing better, the only fair comparison is between you and you.

Let's See What Happened with Lorraine

Lorraine's stroke resulted in her need for a wheelchair, but she gradually improved to the point that she was moving quickly around the brain injury rehabilitation unit where she had been for two weeks. A new client, Gail, was admitted for disabilities after she had a fall and mild brain injury, and Lorraine and she became friends. Two days after Gail arrived, Gail's physical therapist told her that she could stop using her wheelchair and switch to a straight cane for walking. Lorraine got upset. She said "Gail has only been here two days and is already walking! I have been in a wheelchair for two weeks and nobody has told me I could get out of it. What's wrong with me?"

Lorraine did not realize that her own progress with speed and skill in using the wheelchair was excellent for **her**. Lorraine got discouraged because she compared herself to her friend who had a completely different kind of injury. By unfairly comparing herself to Gail, Lorraine undermined her own outlook and did not celebrate her own great accomplishments.

Most persons with brain injury will say they were in bed, maybe unconscious, unable to talk, walk, or do the most basic things on the first day of their injury. If asked how much they could do two or more months later, they will describe that they could get around fairly well, talk, at least partially dress themselves, and feed themselves with a regular diet. How about you? What were you able to do early in your injury? Use the first day after injury for your basis of comparison rather than the days before you were injured as a way to feel better. You will have to admit that you have come a long way since those early days.

Look at the differences in these lists in Box 6.6 when you compared positively. Time for you to congratulate yourself on your progress!

Now read through the items in Exercise C in Box 6.8. Keeping these self-defeating thoughts in mind, complete Exercise D in Box 6.9.

Only when you compare yourself with yourself will you be able to notice the wonderful progress you have made. You can also appreciate your family's efforts only when you try to think about what they are going through since your injury. The bottom line is: Only when you compare yourself to yourself, will you truly be able to see, and reward yourself, for your accomplishments. It is always discouraging to try to be someone you are not.

Another type of outlook or thinking pitfall is having unrealistic expectations. This was covered in more detail in Lesson 5, when we talked about the "supposed to" problem that leads people to feel discouraged and downhearted when trying to cope with the challenges of having a brain injury. Look at Box 6.10 to learn our third "Outlook Pitfall" and how to avoid it.

Now let's look back at *Joe's story*. Joe's story is an illustration of the impact of unrealistic expectations on recovery and feelings about progress after brain injury. Joe's counselors thought he could get a

---

Box 6.8 Exercise C: Comparison with Others
   Are you saying the following kinds of things to yourself?

"Jeff is going back to work after only three months of rehab. I don't have any idea if I can work again, ever. I am a loser."

"Why can't I get better without antidepressant medications? My friend Mary is always in a great mood, and she doesn't take medication."

"Charlie's family is always here to support him. My family hardly ever comes. Even if they all work, they should be here as much as Charlie's family."

If your self-talk sounds like these quotes, you are comparing apples and oranges, and feeling lousy as a result.

Box 6.9 Exercise D: Ask Yourself the Following Questions.

Do I know anyone else who has a brain injury?

Are my friends' or acquaintances' injuries the same as mine?

How is my injury different?

_____

_____

_____

How is my family's situation different from that of families of my friends with brain injury?

_____

_____

job, and a job may have improved his quality of life. Unfortunately, Joe held on to an unrealistic goal of returning to his job he had before his injury. Joe could not do that same old job, but he refused the new job opportunity. As a result of his unrealistic expectations he lost out.

Box 6.10 Five Outlook Pitfalls: How To Recognize and Avoid Them
Pitfall #3. Unrealistic Expectations

Most of us think big. There is nothing wrong with having aspirations and dreams. However, when you are dealing with the significant challenges involved in recovery from brain injury, high hopes can be so high they lead to discouragement. Having realistic, doable goals is the key to developing a positive outlook and self-satisfaction during recovery from brain injury. The business of goal-setting is tricky. If you aim too low, you may sell yourself short and not fulfill all that you are capable of. On the other hand, aim too high, and you are bound to get frustrated and feel bad.

Now complete the questionnaire in Box 6.11 to find out how realistic your goals for recovery are.

If you checked even a few of the items, you are likely to be setting goals that are out of your reach for right now. You could be feeling frustrated and discouraged as a result. Perhaps it is time to use strategies for improving your outlook.

Clearly most people with brain injury want to improve their ability to do activities that are now more challenging for them since their brain injury. Almost everyone has clear goals for their life and recovery. Goals that are doable help people make more progress, feel more confident, and improve the quality of their lives after brain injury. However, goals that are too high can lead people with brain injury to feeling discouraged and badly about themselves.

Zach's Story

Zach's ATV tipped over and, despite wearing a helmet, he had a brain injury. His hospital recovery and rehabilitation are going well. He is weak on one side so he has to wear a small brace on one calf and walk with a 4-pronged cane. Zach is embarrassed when his

---

Box 6.11 "How Realistic Are My Goals?" Questionnaire*
Check Any Items That Sound Like Your Goals For Recovery ...

1. I want to go right back to work. I have had plenty of rehab and am tired of waiting and not earning any money!_____

2. I am aiming for a complete recovery._____

3. I have set lots of goals but have not actually met any of them._____

4. I have been in a rut lately._____

5. I often lose out because I set my goals too high._____

6. I am not sure how to set realistic goals for myself.____

7. I am only interested in attaining my top goal. I won't settle for less._____

*Source: Modified from *Choosing, Finding, and Keeping a Job After Brain Injury* (Niemeier, Kreutzer, & DeGrace, 2009).

girlfriend comes to see him. He hates that he walks unsteadily. The Recreational Therapist invited Zach to come on an outing with a group of clients from the Unit, to go to the bowling alley. Zach declined saying, "My goal is to be the same as I was before my injury. I am not going out anywhere until I can walk without a cane and brace!" When Zach went home, he stayed home, back in his room. He started to get really depressed because his goal was keeping him from opportunities to see friends and get back out doing his favorite activities. If Zach had doable, step-wise goals, he might be out and about instead of sitting in his room.

The Five-Step Goal-Setting Scale

People can get in a habit of thinking that life has only "the best outcome" and "the worst outcome." For the most part, though, almost everything happens in the middle—part good, part not so great. Now we will learn how to use the "Goal-Setting Scale" to improve your ability to set reachable and realistic goals. We will use the following scenario as a sample demonstration.

Sara would like to get a job as a receptionist in an office because she was a receptionist before her injury. Her speech is slow and hard to understand as a result of the brain injury so answering the telephone would be a challenge. Now we will help Sara set a realistic work goal by using the "Goal-Setting Scale" in Box 6.12. We will start at the bottom of the scale with "Worst outcome." What do you think the worst outcome would be for Sara? Probably that she would not

Box 6.12 Goal-Setting Scale—Sara's Goal

Best Outcome	Getting my same receptionist job back
Next Best Outcome	I get a part-time job as a receptionist
Middle Outcome	I work full time as an office mail handler or file clerk
Next Worst Outcome	I work part-time in a retail store as a stock clerk
Worst Outcome	I am not able to get any job

be able to get any job. Now go to the top. What would the best outcome be for Sara? Of course, she would probably think getting her same job back, right? How about the next best, the next worst, and the middle outcome? We have filled in what Sara might tell us.

Using the scale has given Sara more than one goal step. Even if Sara starts out at the "Next Worst Outcome" and works part-time as a stock clerk, she could possibly look forward to moving up over time. She might even continue to advance toward the best outcome. She will feel good about having work of some kind in the meantime, even if it is not her top choice. Any job, and the friends and opportunities it might bring, could lead her closer to her top goal. She also has doable goals along the way.

Now try to think of a goal of your own. Try to write down the goal clearly.

Using the blank "Goal-Setting Scale" (Box 6.13), try the strategy with your goal.

As you fill in each level, notice that there may be smaller successes you could miss if you just aim for the highest step.

Now look at Box 6.14 to learn about our fourth "Outlook Pitfall" and how to avoid it. If you read Amy's story you can see how sneaky and disruptive "awful-izing" thinking can be.

Box 6.13 Goal-Setting Scale

Goal:_____

_____

Best Outcome:

Next Best Outcome:

Middle Outcome:

Next Worst Outcome:

Worst Outcome:

Box 6.14 Five Outlook Pitfalls: How To Recognize and Avoid Them
Pitfall #4. Awful-izing

Awful-izing is a tendency to think of the worse possibilities, no matter what. Even when others point out that something positive is happening or might happen, the person just focuses on the worst or most negative things about their situation.

Consider Amy's Approach

Amy slipped on some wet leaves as she came home with two bags full of groceries in a heavy downpour. She fell backwards and hit her head. She was diagnosed with a traumatic brain injury. It took about one week for her to begin to come out of the confusion she experienced. Soon she noticed that it was harder for her to talk to others and be understood. She had trouble getting nursing and other staff to understand that she had severe pain in her back and head. Panic began to increase and she started telling herself that "This is terrible. This is the worst thing that has ever happened to me. I don't believe I will recover. I might die."

Amy had trouble sleeping because her thoughts created such intense anxiety for her. A chaplain came by and tried to reassure her that she would get better. She felt like God was against her. She told herself she was a hopeless case. She worried that her husband would leave her. She worried that she might not be able to do anything. *"By awful-izing",—or always thinking about the worst outcomes possible,—*Amy put herself in a pit and was unable to see out.

Amy's story shows how the habit of "awful-izing" can take over a person's thinking slowly. Now try the exercise in Box 6.15 to find out if you have a tendency to "awful-ize," and to learn ways to counteract this habit of thinking. Recall a recent or past event or circumstance that was unpleasant or challenging. Maybe you had a painful medical procedure. Maybe you rode the bus for a long time, only to find out that you took the wrong bus and went to the wrong place. Think back about all the details of the situation. Now try to

Box 6.15 Changing the Tendency to Awful-ize

Type 1. Awful-izing	Type 2. Put a Positive Spin on It
This is the worst thing I have ever done!	Looks like I made a mistake. Time to try something else.
My back hurts. I might have a disc problem. Maybe I'm becoming paralyzed.	My back hurts. I should take some pain medicine.
I haven't heard from that employer. I will never be able to work.	I think I will call that employer. It has been a couple of weeks. I can show them I am still interested in the job.
Physical therapy is really hard right now. I don't think I will ever get better.	Physical therapy is tough, but I believe I can get better if I just keep trying.
My memory is horrible! I am worthless now.	I keep forgetting names. Time to use some of those strategies I learned in rehab.

remember what you were saying to yourself at that time. The two columns labeled "Type 1" and "Type 2" in Box 6.15 include examples of things that people might say to themselves as they attempt to improve following brain injury.

Notice how the Type 1, awful-izing statements are deadends and lead nowhere. In contrast, Type 2, positive comments move people toward solutions, and proactive coping. Type 2 comments show what positive thinking can do!

Which column, Type 1 or Type 2, contains statements that sound like what you might be saying to yourself after a difficult circumstance? If you are in the habit of using more Type 1 statements, you may be guilty of awful-izing, and making yourself miserable. Now recall a time when you were trying to do something hard, and noticed the task was very difficult for you to finish. Try to remember as many details of that situation as possible. Take a piece of blank paper and write down any statements you were making to yourself at the time that you can remember. When finished, try to put your statements in the Type 1 or Type 2 column of Box 6.16. See if you are able to Box out which column is the correct one for each of

Box 6.16 Classifying Your Self-Statements

Type 1. Awful-izing	Type 2. Put a Positive Spin on It

your self-statements. Do you have all Type 1's? Do you have any Type 1's?

Next, transform or change all of your Type 1 comments from Box 6.16 into Type 2's in Box 6.17.

From now on, try to transform your Type 1's to Type 2 statements. If you can practice this, you will have a more positive outlook, see a way out of the pit, and feel more in control of your situation.

Box 6.17 Transforming Your Self-Defeating Thoughts into Positive Self-Talk

Type 1. Awful-izing	Type 2. Put a Positive Spin on It

Look now at Box 6.18 to learn about our fifth and final "Outlook Pitfall," and how to avoid it.

The first step, as with the other Pitfalls, is to find out if you are talking negatively to yourself. Try monitoring your self-talk during each day. Try to listen to how you treat yourself, what you say to yourself as you go through your day. Ask yourself, "Am I beating myself up, criticizing myself?" Now we will show you how to use a chart similar to the Type 1 and Type 2 chart in Box 6.16, to start catching yourself in any negative self-talk. Keep a record on an index card whenever you catch yourself making what you think was a negative comment about yourself. Also notice and record any positive self-statements. Using Box 6.19, write your negative self-statements under Type 1 and positive self-statements under Type 2.

Now just as you transformed your "awful-izing" statements earlier, begin to transform your Type 1 self-talk into Type 2 positive self-statements. In Box 6.20, there are some examples to get you started recording and transforming, and enough lines for you to transform your own negative thoughts.

Box 6.19 Stop Negative Self-Talk!

Type 1. Negative Self-Statement	Type 2. Positive Self-Statement

Box 6.20 Transforming Negative Self-Talk

Type 1. Negative Self-Statement	Type 2. Positive Self-Statement
Sample:	Sample:
I can't do this.	I will try my best.
People will laugh at me if I can't remember their names.	Everyone makes mistakes. I can always try again, using my strategies for memory.
No one likes me now or asks me to do things with them.	I will call a friend or two and ask them questions about themselves. Everyone likes to talk about themselves.
Now you try, using your own words:	Now you try, using your own words:

Continue to practice, using this format, until you get better at transforming your negative self-talk into positive self-talk. Practice makes perfect!

Summary

You have learned about and practiced using strategies to avoid five self-defeating habits of thinking that can hinder progress in recovery from brain injury and reduce the quality of post-injury life. Pitfalls 1 and 2 included two kinds of self-defeating comparisons, comparing the pre-injury you and the post-injury you, and comparing yourself and someone else with a brain injury that you know or heard about. Pitfalls 3, 4, and 5 were Unrealistic Expectations, Awfulizing, and Negative Self-Talk. You also took questionnaires to help you see whether you were falling into these thinking pits! You learned a strategy for setting doable, realistic goals; and for recording and then transforming negative thoughts into positive thoughts. As a result of your work in Lesson 6 you are closer to having the most powerful ingredient for successful healing after a brain injury—a nurturing and positive view of yourself and your ongoing progress.

Lesson 7

Thoughts for People in the Life of Persons with Brain Injury

Overview

This Lesson is written *for the people in the life of someone with a brain injury.* The exercises are designed for people who have a relationship to a person with a brain injury. If you are a significant person in the life of someone with a brain injury and are reading this book to learn about them, this Lesson is for you.

For the person with a brain injury reading this Lesson, you will learn about the issues significant people in your life must address as you cope with your injury. It may be difficult for someone with a brain injury to read about the stresses and frustrations those significant to them encounter. Still, imagine you are listening in on their concerns. Be prepared that this Lesson, written for others, is very direct about their needs and issues. Hopefully, if you read this Lesson, it will open a sincere dialog with those significant to you.

Goals for This Lesson

- To explain to people with significant relationships to someone with a brain injury the stresses they may encounter

- To guide spouses/partners, children/parents, friends/employers on handling their unique issues

- To help everyone cope with guilt, frustration, and uncertainty

Common Responses by Significant Others

"My wife seems like a different person now and I have to do the work for both of us in our marriage."

"My fiancée doesn't remember me!"

"None of my friends realize how badly hurt my son is."

"My husband can't handle coming to the hospital to see our daughter."

"We are not formally married, but she is my partner and I know her better than her family whose members won't listen to me."

As these sentiments convey, it can be very difficult when you have a significant relationship to someone with a brain injury and need to adapt to the demands of life after brain injury. A brain injury in someone you have a relationship with will affect *you*. However, it is likely that you are unprepared for the impact of the brain injury on you and your relationship with the person after a brain injury. This is not surprising.

There are three reasons for this:

- Probably no one provided you education about brain injury before it occurred.

- Each injury is different, so it would be hard to prepare for the changes you are likely to experience.

- The health care system focuses on the care of the person with a brain injury and does a poorer job of attending to the needs of the people who have relationships with the person who sustained a brain injury.

So, if you are a spouse, partner, parent, child, friend, or employer of the person with a brain injury, you will find a section of this Lesson relevant to you.

Coping for Those in Relationships

Spouses

Spouses are often in shock immediately after their loved one has a brain injury. As time passes, shock evolves into being overwhelmed and uncertain. Eventually, a sense of loss develops as you become aware of deficits in the person with the brain injury and acknowledge changes in your marital lifestyle that begin to emerge.

As a spouse, your life is proceeding down a different road than you had planned. In Lesson 5, the normal, but detrimental comparisons the person with a brain injury makes with the life that was lost was explained (see Figure 5.1). As a spouse, you are also likely to make the same comparisons. There are two reasons why this is true.

- Little support

  - You may be receiving little support for the impact of the injury on you.

  - You may feel that you are supposed to focus on the needs of your spouse. If you worry about yourself, you may feel guilty since the role you were taught by our society is to attend to the needs of the injured person. (See Lesson 5 for how "should, supposed to, ought to, must, and have to" lead to guilt and anger.)

- Lost hopes

  - Your dreams may be threatened by the brain injury.

  - You may have fears about your future.

Let's try an exercise about having too little support. Hopefully you will better understand how your own needs can get pushed aside.

Exercise

Write down an instance when you felt guilty about your own needs.

_____

_____

_____

_____

_____

How were you telling yourself that you should not be worrying about yourself?

_____

_____

_____

_____

Did other people encourage you to put aside your own concerns? If so, how did they communicate that you should not attend to your own needs?

_____

_____

_____

_____

If it has been awhile since the injury, have you noticed that your friends are drifting away? Write down in what ways you have noticed this happening?

_____

_____

_____

_____

Perhaps you can now see how it easy to get trapped into ignoring your own needs and worries.

- You may find that your friends, family, and employer may inquire about how your spouse with the brain injury is doing, but forget to check on how you are coping.

- Your usual main source of support during most crises, your spouse, is "unavailable" to you because it is your spouse who had the injury.

Just as your awareness of the real-world implications of the injury grows over time, your support system of friends and family moves on with their lives, and you may experience increasing isolation.

If your support system has helped you over time take care of yourself and meet your own needs, then you are fortunate. If not, then it is important that you figure out how to decrease your sense of loss and get support for doing so. There is hope.

It is important that you accept that it is all right for you to be concerned about you. Really. So, the first step is to know what your needs are. Look at the checklist in Box 7.1. Mark the needs that are currently unmet for you.

Once you have identified your needs, figuring out how to get help and information can seem like a daunting process. There are a number of sources of help. First, you can access friends or family members for help.

Friends or family members are much more likely to help than you might first think. The problem they have is that they assume that your needs go *down* over time, just like they would if your spouse had broken a leg. Also, if they are not asked, they assume that things are all right. Ask. Most people care and are willing to pitch in and help, if they understand the extent of your needs.

Asking for help requires you to overcome the hurdle of feeling embarrassed to need help. Remember that no one is prepared for a brain injury and you ought not to expect that you should be able to handle it alone. It is crucial that you avoid feeling embarrassed for needing help. Embarrassment will stop you from seeking the help that everyone needs after a spouse has a brain injury. To solicit help in the most effective manner, you must be comfortable with self-disclosure.

You will get the most help when you make your need personal. Talk about your feeling overwhelmed and afraid. Tell people about your sense of loss. Be specific, too. If you are at risk for

Box 7.1 Checklist of Unmet Needs

Help for you with . . .

☐ Emotional support

☐ Child rearing

☐ Depression

☐ Sleep disturbance

☐ Supervision of your spouse

☐ Job-hunting

☐ Meal preparation

☐ Legal problems

☐ Understanding medical reports

☐ Applying for Social Security

☐ Respite care

☐ Transportation

☐ Other _____

Information about . . .

☐ Brain structure and function

☐ Brain injury mechanisms

☐ Course of recovery

☐ Cognition

☐ Emotions

☐ Behavior

☐ Financial planning

☐ Conservatorship/guardianship

☐ Support groups

☐ Lawyers

☐ Insurance

☐ Other_____

losing your job because you are responsible for transporting your spouse to therapies or a day treatment program every day, tell your friends that. If you are facing money difficulties, see if your friends and family would conduct a fundraiser for you.

- In addition to self-disclosure, you may have to facilitate the education of your friends and family about brain injury. An excellent source of information for you, your friends, and your family is your local state chapter of the Brain Injury Association of America or the national organization itself. Some chapters have printed and videotape information. There are usually educational seminars or conferences for spouses, families, and friends. Remember, in all likelihood they do not appreciate the implications of brain injury. Their knowledge probably comes from misrepresentations perpetrated by erroneous television shows. In those shows, if one blow to the head causes damage, the second blow fixes it!

Second, if you need help and friends or family are unwilling or unable to help, your state Brain Injury Association can often be of assistance.

- Your state Brain Injury Association of America chapter should know who the resources are in your area that help after brain injury. Frequently, there are providers who will help with transportation, respite care, financial planning, etc.

- Ask if your state Brain Injury Association provides case resource facilitation services (a knowledgeable person who can make and coordinate contacts), and if they do, make the most of them.

Third, you can ask your physician, psychologist, social worker, etc., about whom to call for help.

- These professionals typically know of services and agencies that provide a wide array of supportive help.

- Ask for a referral to a specific person at an organization, not just the organization, whenever possible. Quality of service and knowledge about brain injury varies between people at organizations. Also, you will get more personal service when you call someone and say, "I was referred to you personally by so and so who told me to ask specifically for you."

- If your provider is recommending that you contact a large organization or system, rather than a person, it may help if the provider makes an initial call for you to assist you in getting through some red tape. Providers sometimes can smooth the way and get a quicker response from organizations. Providers may also better understand what they are being told on the phone and may think of questions to ask on the phone that you would not think to ask.

- It may work best for you and your provider to make a call together. If you and your provider cannot coordinate calls together, see if your state Brain Injury Association will facilitate the calls for you.

It can be hard to stay organized when asking for help. It is recommended that you make a list of what each person is being asked to do. Box 7.2 provides you with a handy reminder form.

Next, let's look at lost hopes. It is all too easy to not even think about your loss. It is all right to have experienced a sense of loss, and you need not have to deny the impact of the injury on you. While writing down your losses may seem counterproductive, it may relieve you from living with an ill-defined, pervasive grief that you have difficulty addressing. In the following exercise, see if you can capture your sense of loss.

Exercise

What dreams or expectations for the future do you feel you have lost?

_____

_____

_____

_____

_____

What about the brain injury makes you feel this way?

_____

_____

_____

_____

_____

Box 7.2 Assistance Reminder

	People	Item from Box 7.1 Checklist
Family members	_____	_____
	_____	_____
	_____	_____
Friends	_____	_____
	_____	_____
	_____	_____
Brain injury association	_____	_____
	_____	_____
	_____	_____
Professionals	_____	_____
	_____	_____
	_____	_____

Coping with this sense of loss is a two-step process. First, you must determine whether the losses are real. Many people project the future and assume that goals are out of reach. They have "anticipatory grief" in which they grieve for losses that may not occur. It would be best to make inquiries of others about how likely the brain injury will cause you to lose a goal you had.

- Ask experts in the brain injury field how to achieve your goal and cope with the changes imposed by the brain injury. You are likely to find that your situation is similar in at least some ways to scenarios they have seen before. They may have ideas, methods, or resources you might not have thought about.

- Ask people involved in your hopes (e.g., for a career goal that you feel is lost, involve your employer) about how they may be able to help you still reach your dream. Many such people will help more than you might imagine if they are asked.

Use the form in Box 7.3 to write down who you are going to consult with about your hopes.

It is almost taboo to raise the next point, but it bears attention. Spouses sometimes think about leaving the brain injury behind through divorce. You are not a bad person, if you have had thoughts of divorce. When trauma occurs in life and you feel helpless, it is natural to respond by trying to extricate yourself from the situation.

Box 7.3 People to Consult with About My Hopes

Person	Hope/Dream

However, most spouses begin by wanting to have their marriages succeed in the face of brain injury. The challenge is that the roles in your marriage may change:

- Perhaps you are now the main source of income and you may have to begin paying bills.

- Maybe you have to do all of the driving.

- Most of the child rearing may be your responsibility.

Second, to succeed you will need to adjust your expectations for yourself and your spouse. You and your spouse with the brain injury may need to learn new skills. This can be scary. It is all right to be worried about how you will do this. Again, get help; you do not have to do this all alone. Many couples make the necessary adjustments. Learning how to distribute the responsibilities is something you can do, with help.

Partners

Partners face the same issues that spouses do (and so should work through the exercises in the preceding section for spouses), but sometimes with less security. Partners may include boyfriends/girlfriends who have been together a long time, gay and lesbian couples, or people in other relationships. The lower security stems from two factors:

- In some instances, the lack of clear legal standing causes problems. You may find that your access to information is limited by not having legal standing. In addition, without legal standing you may not be allowed to make decisions for the person with a brain injury. Providers can have their hands tied by legal constraints. Laws and the courts may direct professionals about who to give information to and whose desires to follow for decision making. It is worth discussing these concerns with the providers you are dealing with. You may find there can be some sort of accommodation that can be arranged.

- Other people may respond differently to your relationship than you may hope. Family members of persons with a brain injury may assert their belief in their right to make decisions, rather than you. They may try to prohibit you from seeing your injured partner, if they disapprove of the relationship. They may try to exclude you from conferences with providers. If there were conflicts in values or if family members rejected the choices your partner had made, the family dynamics surrounding those differences may play out in front of providers.

Exercise

In what ways have you encountered difficulties with professionals when wanting to be involved?

_____

_____

_____

_____

_____

In what ways have you encountered resistance from family members in being involved?

_____

_____

_____

_____

If your difficulties have been with professionals, then you should be direct with them about your concern.

- If they are unaware of your desires then they should become more inclusive.

  - You may encounter some professionals who fail to appreciate your sense of loss and grief, misjudging the emotional impact upon *you* since you may not appear to them to have either a traditional or permanent relationship.

They may unintentionally disenfranchise your grief. This is unfortunate.

- Explain that your experience of grief is heartfelt and true and it is short-sighted to categorize the emotion of loss by the definition of the relationship. Rather, it is the emotional bonds and the personality of the partners that, in part, drive their emotions.

- Communicating your needs to professionals directly can assist you in obtaining help. Be specific and call attention to unmet needs. Too often, partners assume professionals perceive their needs. Don't rely on such assumptions.

- If they are bound by law or regulation, they may be able to give you suggestions on what steps you need to take to become involved.

- If they cannot see a way to help, then you can consult with their facilities' "Patient Advocate" office to see if there is an overlooked solution.

If your issues are with family members, know that it is very difficult to address these issues when you are already confronted with your partner's brain injury. Typically, partners of persons with a brain injury feel disillusioned, hurt, and angry with family members if those members take actions that seem to deny the partner's emotional ties to the person with a brain injury. Still, while normal, your resentfulness over having to deal with this is harmful to you. It is likely to make you angrier and less effective. The question is not whether you have grounds for being upset, but whether being upset helps you.

There are three approaches you can take:

- The most confrontational approach is legal action. Sometimes partners seek conservatorship/guardianship in direct opposition to the family. Sometimes the family members respond similarly and then a legal battle ensues regarding who will obtain legal decision-making authority. This can be expensive and time consuming. Furthermore, it is often unclear how successful each party will be in court. It is important to realize the impact these disputes can have on the person with a brain injury. From the standpoint of providers, a crucial concern is that the disagreements not be played out *in front of* persons with brain injury, if doing so will affect their recovery and coping.

- The second approach is to engage the providers with whom you are working. If as a partner you were significantly involved in the person's life, providers generally want to be able to gather information from as many sources as is feasible and involve all parties, if possible, in care. Providers may be able to help balance competing interests and act as a buffer between estranged partners and family members. This works only if the desires of different parties are not diametrically opposed. A common example occurs when various parties will not communicate, but all will let information flow to everyone separately from providers.

- The third recourse is the best. Seek compromise with the other significant people in your partner's life. Too often, people let their own emotional needs take precedence over the needs of the person with a brain injury. Sometimes alienated people can come together for a common good. Old battles can be fought about in the future instead of now. People can be surprised at how well they may work together, if they focus on the problems at hand.

Parents of Adult Children

The parents of persons with brain injury typically have to confront an array of issues. Often parents feel guilt over their inability to have protected their child from a brain injury. (Guilt of this nature can also occur when the loved one dies.) After all, parents typically consider their first responsibility to be the physical safety of their children. Brain injury, perhaps the worst damage the body can sustain, rips at people's self-concept as good parents. Yet, professionals know that parents generally could not have prevented the brain injury.

Most activities that lead to brain injury are usually harmless: driving, sports, etc. Most people do not sustain brain injury in most normal activities. So, it is unreasonable to hold yourself to the standard that you should have predicted a low probability event. People cannot live continually afraid of everything that *might*, on an off chance, cause an injury. Hence, the guilt you may experience ("If only I had …) is likely unfounded.

Exercise

In what ways have you been telling yourself that you could have predicted or prevented the brain injury?

_____

_____

_____

_____

In contrast, what messages have you received from other people or professionals to dissuade you from feeling guilty?

_____

_____

_____

_____

Perhaps you would feel better if you listened to the messages others are giving you. It is all right to be gentle on yourself. Harsh judgment is detrimental to you and to your loved one with a brain injury. Your loved one needs you to be involved in the rehabilitation and recovery process, not paralyzed with guilt. You can serve as a compassionate, but logical resource. Your help is needed. Self-recrimination interferes with effective support.

Roles Issues: Nurturer

Your parental role is a difficult one after an adult child has had a brain injury. Some parents re-adopt familiar roles to help cope. One role is resumption of the "nurturing" role you fulfilled when the person with a brain injury was young. This can be a great service.

You may be able to provide housing, cooking, transportation, supervision, etc. You can help absorb some of the burden of care that otherwise might fall on spouses and friends. Still there are risks associated with this role.

- It is easy to burn out if you take on too much of the support load, and if you are feeling guilty you may well overdo it. Remember helping after brain injury is a marathon, not a sprint. You must pace yourself. A 50% percent effort sustained for years is better than 100% effort from which you collapse after six months. (This is true for spouses, too.)

- If you adopt the nurturing role, you should be aware that you may be the target for the frustration of the person with the brain injury. If the role includes setting limits on driving, chemical use, dating, working, independence, cooking, or recreational activities (e.g., snowmobiling, bicycling), you may catch the brunt of the person's anger. Similarly, you may have to enforce compliance with ongoing treatment attendance and recommendations.

- The tendency is to revert to the techniques you used as the parent of a young child. However, this is fraught with problems. Persons with brain injury revolt against being treated like children. Usually they expect to be treated as they were before their injury. However, *you* are aware of their cognitive, emotional, and behavioral issues.

Therefore, you should strive for balance. Provide support: don't smother.

- Seek advice from professionals about what freedoms are permissible and what restrictions are necessary.

- Ask the professionals to take responsibility for promulgating the rules. It is actually best to do this with both you and your loved one present so everyone knows that you are following the professionals' advice and everyone has heard the same thing.

- Ask for written restrictions to decrease misunderstandings.

- Look for specific recommendations to implement the restrictions (e.g., to implement the restriction of "no driving" by the person with brain injury, if impulsivity is an issue or the person disagrees about the driving restriction, you might have the specific recommendation to "keep the key with you at all times").

You can use the form in Box 7.4 to record restrictions and specific recommendations.

How you discuss restrictions with the person with a brain injury is essential.

▪ You must monitor your tone of voice and attitude so that it is an adult-to-adult conversation, while simultaneously being aware of the person's cognitive deficits (e.g., memory, reasoning, judgment, attention span, insight).

▪ You *can* put forth most ideas, if you avoid being either condescending or angry and frustrated.

▪ Remember, you and your loved one are likely under a great deal of stress, experiencing grief and loss. It is best if you can

---

Box 7.4 Restrictions and Recommendation Form

Restriction example: "NO DRIVING"

    Recommendation: "Family to keep keys locked up."

            "Family to keep keys with them at all times."

Restriction 1: _____

    Recommendation: _____

            _____

Restriction 2: _____

    Recommendation: _____

            _____

Restriction 3: _____

    Recommendation: _____

            _____

emotionally prepare yourself for conversations. Take time to mentally and emotionally get ready to discuss issues.

Roles Issues: Breadwinner

Another role that parents sometimes re-adopt is that of "breadwinner." Prior to injury, when your adult child was much younger, you provided financial support as the breadwinner of the family. After a loved one has a brain injury, you may find that your most comfortable reaction is to work longer hours. This is a natural response, particularly among parents who are struggling themselves to cope with the injury. Furthermore, since financial distress often accompanies brain injury due to medical bills and loss of employment by the person with the brain injury, it can be extremely important to supplement income. As with the nurturer role, the breadwinner role requires balance.

- Work can be seductive. It can feel safe and familiar in a world that seems uncertain after brain injury. Brain injury is an ambiguous loss. Work is something you can control, whereas life after brain injury seems chaotic.

- You should be careful to avoid withdrawing from your family and your child with a brain injury. It is too much to expect that you will cope well with brain injury when work isolates you.

- You, too, need the emotional support of your family, just as they need your support.

Roles Issues: Parent of Married Child

A final pitfall bears attention. If your child is married, or in a relationship, you may need to address the desires of the partner and how all of your roles can complement each other. Too often, conflicts arise between spouses (or partners) and parents about what direction care (e.g., rehabilitation, living arrangements, supervision) should take and how to utilize the resources everyone brings to the situation.

It can be challenging to you as a parent to assume a deferential role when your instincts at seeing your child hurt trigger the previous nurturer or worker roles. You may find yourself wanting to take charge. After all, you obviously have the longest relationship with your child and probably have intervened in the past on your child's behalf. Moreover, you bring maturity and life experience to the situation that spouses or partners may lack. Do not be surprised if you find that you are frustrated in your efforts to impart your expertise and to lead your extended family if the spouse wants to be in charge.

Of course, the opposite may arise; you may be requested to step in as others flounder and are overwhelmed. This too can be trying, if it is unexpected. If you had accommodated yourself to your children being adults and making their own decisions, it can be jolting to again need to be in charge. Some parents find it difficult to sacrifice the lifestyle they have with their grown children by being drawn into a more intimate, immediate parenting role again, having to cook, clean, drive, etc., for their now adult child. For some parents this is particularly hard if they had a pre-onset difficult relationship with the spouse or partner. You may feel resentfulness or anger in such circumstances. You may even wonder if the spouse or partner will stick with your child through the turmoil of brain injury.

These are normal feelings. You are not alone in feeling this way. Wanting to take charge, on the one hand, or resenting to do so, on the other, are emotions that professionals often see parents wrestling with. Again, be gentle on yourself for struggling with how to proceed. There is no clear roadmap.

You must be honest with yourself. What do you *want* to do? What do you feel *obligated* to do? What can you *handle* doing?

Exercise

Write down what responsibilities/decision making you want to have.

_____

_____

_____

_____

_____

Write down what responsibilities/decision making you feel obligated to have.

_____

_____

_____

_____

_____

Write down what responsibilities/decision making you can handle having.

_____

_____

_____

_____

The answers to these three questions may very well be in conflict with each other. Your desires, responsibilities, and abilities may not match. You may not want to resume a daily parenting role, feel you are supposed to do so, but not feel able to manage it. You may want to be intimately involved, though not feel you have to, but feel capable of it, if needed. These are numerous combinations of answers to the preceding questions.

The best advice is to seek equilibrium.

■ Discuss your involvement with the professionals working with your loved one. They can impart their experiences with previous families as to what is likely to work and what will be ineffective.

■ Tell the professionals your feelings and any dilemmas; they may be able to help you resolve your conflicting desires.

■ Contact with support groups of other parents who are further post-onset may prove valuable for their insights. (See Lesson 8.)

However, the choice is ultimately yours: you may decide to be very involved; you may elect to be distantly supportive; you may select a middle road. Pick what you believe is best in light of the answers to the three questions discussed above and what you feel is right for your child. See Box 7.5 for a reminder of the crucial questions for your decision making.

Regardless of your decision, do not hesitate to ask for therapy with a psychologist for *you*. Implementation of your plan can be stressful whatever answers you settle upon. You may feel that you should be able to independently cope with the impact on you of the brain injury to your child. After all, you probably raised your child without psychological support and, moreover, you are not the one with the injury. This perspective, however, may limit you.

- It deprives you of available support and decreases your access to information about brain injury.

- It feeds into the myth that family members ought to be able to handle chronic medical conditions (e.g., brain injury, spinal cord injury) in loved ones just they do acute health concerns (e.g., a broken bone) without ongoing support.

Avail yourself of all the support you can without feeling guilty or inadequate for doing so.

Parents of Young Children

Much of the advice for parents of young children is similar to that for parents with adult children (i.e., avoidance of guilt and burnout, getting specific recommendations, going to support groups, and

---

Box 7.5 The Three Crucial Questions

1. What do I want to do?
2. What do I feel obligated to do?
3. What can I handle doing?

receiving counseling). Nevertheless, there are differences and you may encounter some unique experiences.

- You have the lead role in decision making for a young child; they have no spouse or partner. You have the role for advocating for the needs of your child.

- You have a long-term commitment to care for your child.

- You must deal with the school system.

- You must contemplate developmental stages and how they will interact with brain injury.

You may find that your adaptation to brain injury and its accompanying parental lifestyle change is less stable than that of a parent of an adult person with brain injury. As children advance through developmental stages, the expression of their brain injury may alter. This provides you with a continually evolving set of hurdles, requiring different skills from you as your child grows.

You must structure different support systems for yourself as your child grows. For instance, when the person with a brain injury is young, you must be ready to interact with the school system. This is a special challenge because schools vary widely in their knowledge, attitude, and resources for children with brain injury. In some states, the state agency responsible for education is a wonderful resource. For example, in Minnesota, they sponsor training about brain injury for teachers and others in the school system and prepare written material. Again in Minnesota, there is also a private organization to help parents advocate for educational services (i.e., Parent Advocacy Coalition for Educational Rights at www.pacer.org). In some states you may be surprised to learn, as are many parents, that there may be little help available.

Hence, get help from your professional team. Talk with:

- Rehabilitation Professionals

- School Guidance Counselor

- Special Education Teacher

- School Psychologist

- School Principal
- School District Officers
- County Social Worker
- State Brain Injury Association Chapter
- Private Advocacy Organizations
- State Education Agency

Use the form in Box 7.6 to list who you will talk to for help.

Since parents feel an encompassing bond with their children that entails nurturing, instructing, protecting, advocating, etc., and care after brain injury in a young child requires so much more of all of these, the burden can become too much. Yet, society teaches that there should be no burden too great for parents. Those who put forth this idea do so without considering brain injury.

Box 7.6 Resources to Contact

	Person's Name	Phone
Rehabilitation professional		
Guidance counselor		
Special education teacher		
School psychologist		
School principal		
School district officers		
County social worker		
Brain injury association		
Private advocacy organization		
State education agency		
Other		

Brain injury exceeds the limits of most people for solo nurturing, instructing, protecting, and advocating. Yet, no one in society puts an asterisk next to parenting:

PARENTING*

*NORMALLY GIVE IT YOUR ALL,
BUT AFTER BRAIN INJURY GET HELP!

You will cope better with your grief if you solicit assistance.

Adult Children of a Parent with a Brain Injury

It is distressful to see a parent injured. Most people think of their parents as a source of support and a solid foundation for life. It is difficult to contemplate the sense of loss that accompanies the realization that a parent might be unavailable for sustenance. This is particularly true when the loss is abrupt and unexpected, as is typical with brain injury.

In such instances, three factors come into play that may challenge you.

- You must cope with the shock of the injury.

- You may have to become your parent's decision maker.

- Old relationship issues between you and your parent may surface.

It is worth taking a moment to write down your thoughts about each of these variables.

Exercise

Write down what feelings you have at seeing your parent now seeming dependent.

_____

_____

_____

_____

_____

Write down your feelings about being the decision maker for your parent.

_____

_____

_____

_____

Write down what relationship issues you have with your parent that might be a factor.

_____

_____

_____

_____

Let us examine each of these.

First, it can be gut wrenching to see someone who was an independent, self-reliant individual now appear so vulnerable and needy. Too often, people try to focus only on the care needs of their parent without attending to their own sorrow. As they recognize the startling change in their parent, many adult children become weighed down by the emotional trauma to themselves.

- You are not alone if you are feeling stunned by the changes in your parent, uncertain as to how to reconcile the changes with your image of your parent before onset, and grieving the loss of the relationship you had with your parent.

- Remember to seek out emotional support for yourself. It is easy to fall into the trap of believing that, as an adult, you should be able to cope independently with whatever life throws at you.

However, it is very difficult for someone to see a parent suddenly unable to function as before.

- Society offers few role models, little societal support systems, and no training for you for the changes that occur to parents after brain injury. Hence, avail yourself of resources through your state Brain Injury Association or your hospital's rehabilitation psychology department for counseling services.

- You may also find that a parent's injury causes you to rethink your own values and progress in life. You may even see a parent's injury as a reminder of your own vulnerability. These are profound issues. They relate to the choices you have made in your life, the successes and regrets you have, and the type of person you are. There are no bigger things to reflect upon in life and you are being confronted with them with no preparation time. There will be time to contemplate your values and yourself.

- Be easy on yourself. Do not be unfair to yourself by tackling too much emotion at once. Give yourself breathing room to process your feelings.

Second, you may find yourself thrust into the role of decision maker for your parents. This can be very difficult on you. While in our society people are beginning to prepare for that role with elderly parents who are living longer than they used to and will need help later in life, it is not the same as having to do so suddenly after brain injury. Yet, brain injury is one of the frequent causes leading to the need for help.

For example, a common cause of traumatic brain injury is falling, particularly among older people. However, younger parents can also have a brain injury. Most children find it difficult to be the decision maker for parents who may be in the prime of life. Perhaps you are a young adult having to make financial (e.g., liquidate a family business, sell the family home, pay parents' bills) and health care (e.g., do not resuscitate, select a nursing home) decisions for a prime-of-life parent.

Sometimes there is a spouse who takes on the responsibilities for decision making, but there either may be no spouse (or partner) or they may be unable to assume this role due to emotional turmoil, inadequate skills, or lack of knowledge. In such instances, you, as the adult child can find yourself being the ultimate decision maker.

If so, take your time. Get help in figuring out what decisions are urgent and which ones can be made with more thought. Some decisions are very complex and need expert input.

■ You likely have no prior knowledge about brain injury, courses of recovery, and treatment/placement options. You can avoid misjudgments by learning from the experience of others conveyed through rehabilitation providers. Consult with them.

■ You may face issues related to your parent's insurance, finances, health care directives, etc. Again your rehabilitation professionals or state Brain Injury Association can provide you with information on lawyers and financial planners who specialize in such issues after brain injury.

Third, you may have pre-onset relationship issues between you and your parent that are brought to the surface by the injury. *Be assured that you are not alone in this regard.* The injury may raise numerous issues regarding old resentments, differences in values, lack of respect, etc. It can prove very challenging to cope simultaneously with old issues and new ones raised by the injury. However, it is easier when you are honest with yourself about your old feelings and how the injury impacts them.

Perhaps you feel the opportunity is lost now to resolve old hurts. Alternatively, maybe you feel that this is a chance to reconnect. Regardless, you ought not to be surprised when the injury churns up your emotions. Take this as a chance to evaluate your perspectives and see if they still fit the new situation. This need not be done quickly, however. As discussed above, take the time to sort things out.

Friends

Friendship after brain injury is a challenge. The person with a brain injury may think differently, act differently, and feel different. Your friend may:

■ Be unable to participate in some of the pursuits that you did together before the injury (e.g., contact sports)

- Be restricted from doing particular activities (e.g., alcohol consumption)

- Have symptoms (e.g., fatigue) that may interfere with participation in activities

- Not be able to drive

- Not be able to talk or understand well

- Act in a way that embarrasses you (e.g., social inappropriateness)

So, you may feel torn. You may experience regret at the loss of the relationship you had before the brain injury, while feeling sympathy for your friend's situation; simultaneously, you may feel unsure about how to maintain a friendship with this altered person, experiencing guilt if you decrease involvement.

The typical pattern is early involvement with decreasing involvement as time passes: most people with brain injury lose most of their friends over the years. As your life advances (i.e., career, marriage, children), your friend with the brain injury's life course may be quite different, with decreasing shared life experiences.

What to do?

- It is likely that your friend's injury will be a time of exploration for you of *your* needs, *your* values, and *your* capabilities. Take this as a time of self-reflection, not driven by guilt or other people's expectations, but by your own desire to understand yourself. In this way, let the brain injury provide some good.

- If you can invest in long-term support of your friend with the injury, do so.

- It is all right to be intensively supportive early and to be less so as time progresses. This is common.

- It is all right to grieve for your friend and not be able to handle being involved very much. This does not make you a bad person; it makes you normal.

- It is all right to be confused. After all, usually everyone surrounding a person with brain injury is uncertain early on.

Do what you can for your friend and be honest with yourself about what you can do. There are no wrong choices.

Employers*

Many people lose their jobs after brain injury. This is unfortunate since so many people tie their self-worth to their job. A number of scenarios arise:

- Some persons with brain injury return to work too soon before sufficient cognitive skills return, whereas if they had waited longer, particularly during the first year after injury, for more cognitive recovery, it may have gone better.

- The employer feels that the position cannot be kept vacant long enough because of the need to have the work completed.

- The employer feels that they are unable to design accommodations that would facilitate return to work.

- The job is truly beyond the altered capabilities of the employee.

- The employer is insufficiently committed to the employee to help address the brain injury.

As an employer, there are many types of relationships you might have had with the person who sustained the brain injury. These include close colleague, supervisor of a valued employee, instructor of a sub-par performer, etc. The relationship you had with your employee will likely color your own emotional responses to the brain injury. ***However, most of the time the challenge for the employer is to manage conflicting emotions.***

Suppose the employee is a trusted company leader now unable to perform. Do you feel an obligation to the person and, simultaneously, remorse at the corporate decision you face if the person cannot perform? Imagine the employee was a problem worker. Do you experience both relief at the person's inability to return to work and

---

* All employers should be aware of the requirements of the Americans with Disabilities Act, its Amendments, and any other related laws. Nothing stated here is intended to give advice contrary to any law as it relates to persons with brain injury, and the authors support adherence to all relevant laws.

guilt over your feelings? Yours is not an easy role as human being and employer.

As with other people in the life of the person with brain injury, you face juggling compassion and reality: your emotions and competing demands. What do you feel best doing and what can you handle? There are no clear answers.

However, unlike family and friends who may attend to their expectations for themselves, discounting the limits of what they are really capable of providing long term, employers tend to focus on the "reality" of work, failing to attend to the emotional cost to themselves of the choices they make. As with everyone else discussed in this book, your employee's brain injury presents you with an opportunity to discover yourself. If you focus just on the issue of return to work, you may find yourself emotionally distressed.

Perhaps it is worth it to be explicit about your competing drives.

Exercise

Write down what you would like to do for your injured employee.

_____

_____

_____

_____

_____

Write down what you feel you must do for your business.

_____

_____

_____

_____

_____

If the above exercise highlights conflict, take time to reflect on your abilities to help and to run your business. There are no wrong decisions. Each solution *is* different. Some persons with brain injury cannot return to their old jobs; some can return with help. Some employers, just like other normal people, cannot handle brain injury; others can.

There is one final thought to bear in mind. If you are unable to have the employee return to your company, you might still be of help. After all, most employers articulate to their employees that they do not want just a "do the work — here is your paycheck" relationship. When a brain injury happens to one of your employees, it is an opportunity to demonstrate to that employee and all of your other employees what you meant by truly following through on your idea of a broader relationship.

You might consider developing an ongoing supportive involvement with the person with a brain injury, apart from being an employer. This might help your own sense of loss and be a boon to the person with a brain injury. Imagine: "My boss couldn't take me back to work, but my boss became involved in my life, becoming a friend, emotional confidant, and advocate."

Summary

Brain injury affects everyone. It alters relationships with spouses, parents, friends, employers, etc. Moreover, as an individual in a relationship (spouse, partner, parent, friend, employer) with the person with a brain injury, it will change *you*. You will be affected by the injury in ways you are likely unprepared for. It is best to be honest about the impact on your thoughts and feelings, aware of your own needs, and realistic about how you can help. Provide what help you can; care for yourself; do not feel guilty. Everyone gives to the degree they can. There are many "hidden heroes": people who work on behalf of someone with a brain injury. Take pride in your efforts and also take care of yourself.

Lesson 8   *Getting Support*

Overview

This lesson is intended to educate you about the support you can get from other people apart from the help you receive through professional counseling, family, and friends. The goal is to address hurdles you may feel about seeking support from other people. This Lesson will explore the types of support available and the advantages of pursuing such support. It will prepare you to seek support and explain how to go about it.

Goals for This Lesson

- To explore shortcomings you may have in your support network

- To learn what a support group can provide you

- To understand what to look for in a support group

- To prepare for going to a support group

- To know what other options you have

Common Responses to Support Groups

"I don't want to hear about other people's problems."

"I am uncomfortable telling other people about me."

"No one at the meeting will be like me."

"All they will want to do there is complain."

"Guest speakers usually do not address my situation."

Most people who contemplate going to a support group, or who actually go to a meeting, express sentiments similar to those above. This should not be surprising because going to a support group is a further leap into the unknown of coping with a brain injury. Yet, support groups can be a tremendously powerful tool for recovery, both for you and your family (or friends). In Lesson 3 the focus was on obtaining professional help. This Lesson focuses on using other resources.

The power of using support group resources can be seen in some typical statements from support group participants. Contrast the following feelings with those documented above:

"I realize that my problems are familiar to other people at my group. It makes me feel less odd."

"I am so at ease talking with people at my group. They understand me."

"I have learned that we all share similar experiences."

"In my group, if someone has a complaint or problem, we give them the opportunity to gain perspective and generate solutions."

"I like that my group chooses guest speakers together, so that all of our members can hear speakers that address their needs."

As you can see, those who attend support groups have found that the feelings at the start of this Lesson often prove to be false. This Lesson will help you find a support group that will make you, too, believe in their benefit.

What Is a Support Group?

Support groups exist for lots of different purposes. These reasons include emotional support, social activity, education, referral information, etc. Some groups may meet multiple needs.

However, you may find yourself uncertain as to exactly what needs you want to meet by attending a group until you start going. Then, you may decide that a different style of group than the one you first chose is better for you. Be aware, however, that for many people, and groups, focusing on education and social activity are less threatening than addressing emotional needs, but directly discussing emotions can be the most important service of a group. Be careful to avoid selecting a group that allows you to hide from the therapeutic benefits of emotional exploration by only pursuing other activities.

It is likely to be beneficial to write down what needs you have that a support group might meet.

Exercise

Which of the following are things (check them off) that you wish were available to you?

☐ Sympathetic, but knowledgeable ear about my issues

☐ Emotional release

☐ Guidance on what works for specific problems

☐ Cognitive compensation strategies and applied "Tricks of the Trade"

☐ Social outlet

☐ Information about brain injury

☐ Information about resources, professionals

☐ Information about finances, insurance, funding

☐ Other:

_____

_____

_____

_____

In an ideal world, your pre-existing support network of friends and family could meet all of your needs. Yet, many people who experience brain injury find that this is not so. Your support network may be under considerable stress itself as its members adjust to your injury. Also, your family members may focus on your immediate needs such as physical care, transportation, financial resources, etc., and be too overwhelmed to additionally attend to your emotional needs.

As time progresses, you may see friends moving on with their lives and being less available to you. Furthermore, family and friends, who are unlikely to be familiar with brain injury before your injury, probably lack the knowledge to offer you education and referral information.

Even when people are available to support you emotionally, their suggestions can sometimes be unhelpful. Comments such as "You should feel lucky to be alive" or "If you try harder you can do it" can be counterproductive since such comments can feel like they invalidate the struggles you may be facing.

The idea that "You have to accept this" may be frustrating in that (1) it fails to tell you *how* to reach acceptance, and (2) implies that acceptance after brain injury is easy to achieve. Finally, many people you know may have their *own* need for you to be okay and that may influence their ability to support you when you are not okay.

If you feel that perhaps there is something out there that could help in ways different from your current support network, maybe your current support system has fallen victim to common shortcomings such networks experience.

Exercise

■ Do people in your support network sometimes not know what to say or do?

■ Are people shying away from your situation because it makes them feel uncomfortable?

■ Are some people finding it emotionally painful to see you hurt and not cured?

■ Has anyone in your support system recommended that you go to a support group?

If yes, write down what reasons they gave you?

_____

_____

_____

_____

_____

Perhaps the reasons they gave you hint at the shortcomings they see in your current support system or in their own abilities to help you more.

People have a need to see other people overcome life obstacles. This may stem from their own insecurities about feeling vulnerable to injury themselves. In the same fashion that no one likes to talk about death, people sometimes find that those with a disability remind them of their own mortality: we all prefer to live comfortably with an "invulnerability myth" — it can never happen to us!

Of course, there are lots of truly supportive family and friends. In truth, when they are able to provide emotional nurturing and help, they are likely to prove to be your best source of encouragement. Even during the rehabilitation hospitalization phase of your recovery discussed in Lesson 3, family and friends can afford you support different from that of professionals:

- They know you more intimately and can connect with you more personally.

- You have built up trust with them over years.

Still, even if you have a wonderful network, support groups can supplement their efforts; if you do not have a network that functions well, support groups can facilitate your recovery.

What You can Gain from a Support Group

You may question what you will gain by going to a group: the answer is a feeling of normality! Remember, literally millions of people have brain injuries. Yours is a common condition. The fact that so far you may have met people who know little about brain injury does not alter the truth that so many people either have had brain injuries or are family members, friends, neighbors, co-workers, etc., of persons with brain injury. You are not alone, despite feeling that way sometimes, and a support group can help you realize that.

- A support group can serve as a place where you need not feel defensive about your injury or its impact (e.g., being forgetful, not working, getting divorced). At your group you will not have to cover up problems; you can relax, be yourself, and feel all right. Support groups allow you to dispel guilt and anxiety.

■ Support groups afford you the opportunity to obtain feedback. Since the other support group attendees are not otherwise in your life, you can receive their unbiased feelings about your ideas and plans. Honesty is invaluable and hard to find.

■ Because the members of the support group share your brain injury experience, they will want you to do well. Support group members care about each other.

■ As you continue in your group you will discover that you, too, can offer guidance and help to other people, something that will make you feel good about yourself!

Topics Addressed by Support Groups

Support groups address numerous issues. It is impossible to list them all. Box 8.1 is a checklist that provides examples of reoccurring topics that people often seek help for from support groups. There are spaces at the bottom of the list to add concerns that you might want to raise for discussion at your next support group meeting. If you have an additional concern that is not already on the list, then other people in your group probably have a similar concern and will appreciate you bringing up the topic. Otherwise, you can just check off topics as your group discusses them. Doing so may help you recall the discussions when you are outside of your group.

What They are Not

You should keep in mind that support groups are not a replacement for professional help. There are times when serious issues of adjustment arise (depression, fear/anxiety, mistrust/paranoia, suicidal/self-injurious ideation or behavior, significant guilt and anger, loss of self-esteem, marital discord, aggression, etc.) that require professional insight, knowledge, and resources. Still, support groups can be a wonderful adjunct to counseling or, for many, a sufficient means of support.

Box 8.1 Support Group Topics

_____ Guilt about onset

_____ Anger at family/friends

_____ Successes you are proud about

_____ Money concerns

_____ Role changes

_____ Guardianship issues

_____ Fear when recovery slows

_____ Fatigue

_____ Acceptance

_____ Chemical use (alcohol/street drugs)

_____ Dating and sexuality

_____ Return to work worries

_____ How to tell other people about your injury

_____ Medications

_____ Marital issues

_____ Child rearing

_____ Loneliness

_____ Wishing you had died

_____ Depression

_____ Shame

_____ Fear of another injury

_____ Medical complications/issues

_____ Communication with professionals

_____ Loss of friends

_____ Housing

_____ Transportation

_____ Loss/grief

_____ Other _____

_____ Other _____

_____ Other _____

Support groups are an inappropriate place for romance. You should avoid going to a group with plans to make dating contacts. Group members want to feel secure and safe. The group is a support group, not a singles club. You may make other people uncomfortable if you solicit them.

Of course, friendships do develop out of support groups. That is one of their benefits. However, dating and romance introduce complications. If your relationship goes badly, you risk losing your support group, too, because it can become awkward to attend if your ex-dating partner is there. Even if your relationship goes well, and you both continue to participate in the same group, your relationship will change how you act and what you say during the group.

Hence, do not take your support group resource lightly by assuming that it would be easy to replace. Your support group members are an important resource for you: be careful not to squander that resource.

What To Look for in a Support Group

Telling you what you will find most satisfying in a support group would presuppose that everyone's needs are the same. Actually, the diversity of needs is as broad as the circumstances and effects of brain injury. In addition, your needs may change over time. Nevertheless, there are variables that you can consider when selecting a support group. Each person can individually decide how to rate each support group on each variable.

Type of Members

There are two types of groups:

- Persons with brain injury only (often called a "peer support group")

- Mixed groups that also include family members

The primary advantage of a peer-only group is that it provides you the opportunity to have unvarnished discussions.

- You can discuss issues that you may have *with* your family or concerns you may have *for* your family.

- You may be angry or disappointed with your family and you may want a place where you can vent those feelings.

- You may be worried about your family members and how they are doing.

- A group without family members can provide you with an avenue to express your fears safely.

There are advantages also to a mixed group.

- You can hear how other families are handling issues.

- You may learn that your family issues are common.

- Your family, if they attend with you, may see how other persons with brain injury and their families function, giving them a new perspective on their interactions with you.

- Your family may hear concerns raised by other people, but important to you, without you having to introduce the topic, while opening the door for you to have a discussion with your family. The group discussion can give you and your family a common jumping off point for future private talks (e.g., "Remember what was said at the meeting last week by Sally? I feel the same way sometimes.").

Obviously, you need not choose between these two groups. You could attend one of each for different needs. Be aware that your family may want to also attend a family-only group without you. It is best to avoid being hurt by this. Recognize that they have needs, too, and may want privacy to care for themselves.

Group Facilitator Qualities

Support groups can be run by a:

- Professional

- Family member

- Person with a brain injury

There is no clear answer to this question as to who is best. In part, it depends on whether the group is for families or persons with brain injury, for educational purposes or for support, for help early or late in recovery, etc. Each type of facilitator (professional, family member, or person with brain injury) potentially brings strengths and limitations to the facilitator role. You should reflect on who you will feel most comfortable running your group. In each category of facilitator there are excellent facilitators, and there are those who are limited in their abilities to facilitate a group.

Next, you should determine the qualities of the support group facilitator that best appeal to you. Typically, most people want a facilitator who is experienced, knowledgeable, supportive, not too directive, but able to facilitate communication. You may find it useful to inquire about any training the facilitator has had in running a support group (e.g., instruction through your state chapter of the Brain Injury Association of America).

Most groups function best when facilitators avoid trying to obtain *their* emotional support through the groups they facilitate. Facilitators ought to be able to serve the needs of their groups without their own needs interfering.

Box 8.2 provides a brief checklist of facilitator characteristics to consider. It is all right to ask facilitators about their style, experience, and knowledge; you could even show them this list.

Of course, it may be difficult to fully determine all of the information in Box 8.2 before going to a few meetings, though you may obtain an impression of facilitators by talking with them first. Still, the list can help guide your impressions after a few meetings. It may be useful to attend different groups to see which facilitator feels most comfortable to you.

Group Structure

Some groups attempt to structure meetings, whereas other groups are open-ended. Groups with structure may aim to address topics sequentially across meetings, or they may structure time within a meeting (e.g., if a speaker is coming). The advantage of having structure is that the group insures it will cover important topics that otherwise might be missed.

Box 8.2 Support Group Facilitator Variables

Background

- ☐ Professional
- ☐ Family member
- ☐ Person with a brain injury

Personal

- ☐ Nonjudgmental of other's decisions
- ☐ Tolerant of diversity
- ☐ Seeks to include everyone
- ☐ Nondirective
- ☐ Empathetic and perceptive
- ☐ Positive and enthusiastic
- ☐ Good role model
- ☐ Coping well (if family member or person with brain injury)
- ☐ Not depressed or anxious
- ☐ Receives own support outside of your group
- ☐ Mature

Knowledge

- ☐ Experienced with group processes/communications
- ☐ Understands boundaries and confidentiality
- ☐ Knows purpose and limits of support groups
- ☐ Has long-term commitment to the group
- ☐ Aware of resources
- ☐ Understands brain injury
- ☐ Skilled at keeping group focused
- ☐ Brain Injury Association trained

Open-ended groups are more likely to pursue the immediate needs of its members within meetings or across meetings. Pertinent frustrations or concerns can be more quickly addressed. However, topics that are worrisome, but that no one immediately raises, may get overlooked.

Of course, group structure can change over time and some groups combine structured and unstructured time. Either group is fine; it is personal preference.

Practical Considerations

There are practical considerations when you select a group, too.

- The location of the group may be worth investigating. Some groups meet at hospitals; some groups meet at religious sites. You must decide if you are comfortable in these locations.

- You may need to find out whether the building the group meets in is accessible if you have mobility variables to consider.

- You should determine whether the time of day and day of the week are convenient for you; a great support group that you do not actually attend is worthless.

- You may have transportation needs that are a factor.

- Duration of meeting: too long and you may fatigue; too short and little is addressed.

- Frequency of the group meeting can be a consideration: too often and it can be difficult to attend; too infrequent and it might not meet your needs.

- Ask about donations, if any, to maintain the group (e.g., postage for mailing announcements, copying notices, refreshments).

Box 8.3 provides a checklist of factors for you to mark off as you select a group.

Box 8.3 Practical Support Group Considerations

Location

☐ Hospital   ☐ Religious Site   ☐ Community/Public Space   ☐ Other

Building Accessibility

☐ Accessible   ☐ Not Accessible

Transportation

☐ Self   ☐ Family   ☐ Supported   ☐ Public   ☐ Friend
☐ Times available: _____

Meeting times

☐ Day of Week: _____
☐ Time of Day: _____AM/PM
☐ Duration: _____Minutes
☐ Frequency: _____

Donations

☐ Voluntary   ☐ Required
☐ Amount $_____

How Soon Should You Go?

Hopefully you received information about support groups during your initial rehabilitation. In fact, many professionals anticipate that you will want to go shortly after discharge.

■ You may find that connecting with other people early is a great source of comfort and reassurance.

For some people this may be unrealistic.

■ You may feel too overwhelmed following discharge to add a support group meeting to your agenda.

■ You might need some time out of the hospital to see what life will be like – and what challenges you will face – and how you feel about things.

It is okay if you do not go right away, but professionals tend to be concerned that if you fail to start soon you will never get around to going at all or that you will forget to arrange to go. If you do not start in a group shortly after hospital discharge, it is a good idea to plan a time when you will re-visit going, perhaps about six months after rehabilitation hospital discharge.

By six months you should have some idea of how you are feeling and whether your network is supplying you with all of your support needs. Then, if you choose not to start going to a support group, you should revisit this idea every six months for a few years. It would be a good idea to write down in Box 8.4 the dates to consider a support group.

Note that not everyone with a brain injury has been hospitalized. Some people are seen at emergency rooms and are released. Other people never go to an emergency room. If you are one of these people with a brain injury, you too can contemplate going to a support group. The benefits are awaiting you, also. When you choose to go depends on your personal situation and needs.

Box 8.4 Support Plan

Discharge Date: _____

6 Months Date: _____

12 Months Date: _____

18 Months Date: _____

24 Months Date: _____

You may feel some fear when you think about attending a support group. Reflecting ahead of time about a few issues may relieve much of your anxiety. Remember, everyone there has had a brain injury or knows someone who has one, and while their exact circumstance may not be precisely the same as yours or your family, they likely share many of your experiences. Moreover, even if you had unique experiences, the people at the group are there, in part, to help you. They came, just as you will, to learn, but also to help.

You may be worried about your ability or desire, at least initially, to disclose personal information and feelings. You may feel uncomfortable talking in front of other people. These are normal concerns. You should know:

■ You are not obligated to talk or disclose information, though the group may ask you to introduce yourself. You can tell the group, particularly for the first meeting, that you are nervous and want to get more comfortable before participating a lot.

■ You may discover a desire to participate earlier than you might anticipate when you observe how comfortably the group handles issues just like the ones you confront.

■ As time progresses your hesitancy may decrease as you become familiar with your group members.

Still, if self-disclosure is a particular worry of yours, discuss it ahead of time with the group facilitator. Find out what the ground rules are: does everyone have to talk?

Why People Stop Going to a Support Group

People tend to drop out of support groups. Perhaps you can avoid this pitfall if you know beforehand the reasons that lead some people to stop attending so that you can be ready to side step those traps:

■ You should avoid the illusion that a support group will immediately make you feel better. Becoming more resilient takes time and it requires real life practice of the insights you gain at meetings. In fact, personal self-disclosure, listening to others, and gaining insight can be emotionally painful. On the whole, you should find a support group to be "supportive," but there can be meetings that are emotionally trying.

- You will likely find support groups to be disappointing if you are looking for people who will feel sorry for you. You will find empathetic people, but not people who readily tolerate self-pity. Therefore, some people leave groups because they are unready to transition from despair to acceptance.

- Some people stop attending support groups because they do not want to be with other persons with brain injury. They may find it too hard to see other people with disabilities. They may learn about problems they did not know could occur. They may not be ready to admit how similar to "those people" they are. Attending a support group entails some degree of acceptance (as defined in previous lessons). Of course, if you are struggling with denial, then a support group may be just the place for you to get help with acceptance.

- You may quit a support group because you are afraid to trust, but attending a support group involves trust. If you are going to disclose your concerns (e.g., fears, worries) and your successes, then you need to believe the support group members will treat you gently and support you.

- You may feel lonely and want just the social aspect of a group, but you may find that the emotional discussions are too intense.

- You may find that there was just not a good match of personalities in a particular group.

If these reasons for leaving your group fit you, do not give up on support groups. Rather, locate a new group where you fit better and can trust the people in the group.

Of course, logistical concerns can also influence attendance.

- It can be challenging to arrange reliable transportation.

- Periodic medical flare-ups could interfere too much.

- Other life responsibilities (e.g., work) could conflict with meetings.

- You could struggle with fatigue.

- It may be too much to add in one more appointment.

Whatever your issues in this regard it would be wise to contemplate how you can structure things so as to maximize your attendance.

You may also discontinue attendance because you obtained what you needed from the group.

- You received the information you needed to resolve particular issues.

- You came to sufficient terms with your injury for now.

- You re-established a personal support network that meets your needs.

Of course, some of the people who leave groups periodically return when life circumstances change. Alternatively, they may leave their support group to join other ones because they need a different type of group providing a different experience; maybe they are at different points in their lives now then when they started in their groups. Finally, some people discontinue going to a support group to start their own group as a facilitator.

Whatever your reasons are for leaving a group, you should avoid feeling guilty about doing so. It *is* difficult to succeed in life with a brain injury. Whether your reasons for stopping are logistical or interpersonal, give yourself credit for doing the best you can. Life after brain injury is an experiment: you need to figure out what works best for you. Perhaps a different group would be better for you or a group sometime in future (or maybe support groups are just not for you). Regardless, make an informed decision and be satisfied with your choice.

Individual Peer Support

You may find that a group environment is not for you, but that you would like to talk with someone else with a brain injury. You may be looking for a "peer mentor." A peer mentor is someone you establish a relationship with beyond just being friends. It is like having someone to talk with who has more experience with brain injury than you have and has reached a level of comfort and coping with brain injury. Whereas professional counselors can impart wisdom to you from having seen what worked for many other people with brain injury, peer mentors impart insight from their personal experiences. If they have been successful in coping, then peer mentors can serve as role models for you.

You should use the same care in selecting a peer mentor as you would when screening a support group facilitator. Consider the variables in Box 8.5.

It is best if you arrange for a peer mentor through an organization so that you have some assurance that the mentor is reputable and has your best interest at heart. You want someone who (1) has been trained as a mentor, and (2) is emotionally doing well. You can start by making inquiries at your local hospital or your state Brain Injury Association.

A peer mentor, a professional counselor, and a support group are different resources for you. They are not mutually exclusive—you can have all or any combination as resources at any time.

The Brain Injury Association

Regardless of whether you attend a support group, it is wise to join your state Brain Injury Association. These chapters of the non-profit Brain Injury Association of America can provide support, networking, advocacy, referral, and information. Ask to be placed on their mailing list for newsletters and announcements. You will probably be amazed at the assistance and support the people at the state Brain Injury Association can provide you.

Box 8.5 Peer Mentor Variables

Personal

- ☐ Gender
- ☐ Ethnicity
- ☐ Time since injury

Commitment

- ☐ Frequency of meeting
- ☐ Availability by phone
- ☐ Available for at least one year

Approach

- ☐ Nonjudgmental of other's decisions
- ☐ Tolerant of diversity
- ☐ Empathetic and perceptive
- ☐ Positive and enthusiastic
- ☐ Good role model
- ☐ Coping well
- ☐ Not depressed or anxious
- ☐ Receives own support outside of relationship with you
- ☐ Mature

Knowledge

- ☐ Understands boundaries and confidentiality
- ☐ Knows purpose and limits of peer mentor
- ☐ Has long-term commitment to you
- ☐ Aware of resources
- ☐ Understands brain injury
- ☐ Brain Injury Association trained/screened

The Internet

Some people seek support over the internet in online chat rooms or groups. You should be extremely cautious about online support activities. You must protect yourself. After all, you are seeking support at a time when you may be emotionally vulnerable and it is easy for someone to take advantage of you. You can be emotionally harmed by anonymous people who have hidden motives. Some people on the internet may also try to financially abuse you, and if you ever arrange to meet in person, you can be hurt physically.

It is probably best to attend support groups that are real, not virtual, and that are recommended by recognized organizations (e.g., your local hospital or your state Brain Injury Association). However, sometimes a recognized organization may run a support group over the phone by conference call. Make sure that the organization is reputable (i.e., check with your local hospital or your state Brain Injury Association).

There is, however, some excellent information about brain injury available over the internet. Still, you must be cautious about what you believe. *Anyone* can put information online. A fancy website with great graphics and an official sounding name does not mean the information is accurate. Some people online have an axe to grind or just do not know what they are talking about.

Nevertheless, the internet is valuable. First, it can help you generate questions to ask your professionals or it can raise issues that you can bring to your support group. Second, there are some sites that you can feel more secure in trusting. Good places to start would be your state Brain Injury Association website or the Brain Injury Association of America website (as of this writing, www.biausa.org).

Accepting Your Family Going to a Support Group

One last thought: even if you choose to defer attending a support group, your family members may feel that it is helpful for *them* to go to a group. This varies from family to family.

Why would your family want to go to a support group? It may help them when they:

- Feel scared and need reassurance

- Are angry and need support

- Need to take a little time to care for themselves

- Need validation of their decision making

Of course, just like you, they may want to wait awhile:

- They may be juggling work, child rearing, visits to the hospital, meeting with lawyers, etc.

- It may be too overwhelming to add a support group.

Finally, you should be aware that it may be difficult for your family members to go to a support group, even one just for them.

- The idea of a support group may challenge their sense of competency. They may find it hard to admit their own neediness. Going to group may heighten their own sense of vulnerability. They may be afraid that they will fall apart emotionally, after learning to be strong for you, once they are in an environment where it is all right to admit to their own feelings.

- Guilt can be a big factor that reduces support group attendance by family members. Some family members may feel guilty about spending time caring for themselves, believing that they should focus all of their energy on you. Such family members typically have adopted the role of "nurturer" after your injury. However, without support they risk burn out.

- Other family members feel guilty about not having been able to protect you from harm in life and support group attendance would entail confronting their feeling of having failed you. Such family members often have adopted the role of "provider" after your injury. They may compensate for their perceived failure to protect you by working extra hours at their jobs to help with the bills. They may try to marshal resources to be better able to shield you from the impact of your injury on your life and from harm in the future. However, they risk feeling inadequate without support.

- If family members were angry with you over your pre-onset lifestyle or other factors, they may feel remorse about not having had a better relationship with you before your brain injury. Perhaps they now regret their anger, or even their disappointment with your life choices, and cannot face their own shortcomings in their relationship with you. They may fear that a support group will bring forth their regrets (maybe in tearful self-disclosure). Such family members risk depression without support.

- Apart from guilt, some family members may have feelings of tremendous loss themselves. Family members who were proud of you and had invested in your accomplishments may actually experience a blow to their own ego and esteem. Moreover, if they participated a lot in your life, the gap left in their lives if you are greatly changed, can be a source of uncertainty for them about how to live now. These family members may be embarrassed to disclose such feelings; it is difficult to admit how much of their happiness and satisfaction depended on you. However, these family members risk feeling empty without support.

For your part, it may be surprising to think about issues of guilt, loss, and coping by your family. The preceding paragraphs may even have brought up some uncomfortable thoughts, but don't awful-ize! Put a positive spin on it. First, your family's feelings belong to them and you are not responsible for that. Second, what is done is done: you cannot fix the past, but you can work together to have a better future together. Third, there is help available to your family. Encourage them to attend a support group for themselves!

Summary

Regardless of how you get support (personal network, support group, peer mentor, professional counseling, etc.), you need to remember that you are not alone. Brain injury happens to huge numbers of people every year. However, it gets little newspaper space or television time and what is conveyed by the press is often misleading. It is easy to come to believe that literally no one else has had any of your experiences or could understand your worries. However, that is an error. There are lots of people ready to help you. Reach out: they are there.

Lesson 9   *How to Keep on Recovering Well*

Overview

There are three purposes of this Lesson. First, Lesson 9 will help you integrate all you have learned and discovered through reading this book and participating in the process of self-discovery through its multiple exercises. Second, Lesson 9 should help you (a) combine and prepare to apply both the facts and skills related to recovering from and living with brain injury, and (b) use your awareness of your unique profile of strengths and weaknesses. Third, Lesson 9 will help you think about and formulate a personal plan for maintaining and strategically using your injury-related knowledge and the multiple strategies and coping methods demonstrated and recommended in this book.

Goals of This Lesson

- Describe your personal profile of post-injury strengths and weaknesses

- Identify which of the many strategies you have learned will help each individual challenge

- Maintain a consistent, positive inner voice during the challenges now and in the future

- Describe the network of persons and resources available to you in your community and nation as you continue to recover

Recovering Well!

You have probably read your book all the way to this point and may now wonder whether we will tell you that your challenges are over. Unfortunately, we would have to say that no because, for most people with brain injury, the challenges continue. However, reading the book and completing the exercises has led to increased awareness and understanding that will help your continued recovery. Now Lesson 9 will help you review, integrate, and apply all that you have learned so far. Lesson 9 will also introduce and present the combined wisdom of many persons in the community with brain injury, some of whom have lived with it for many years. This wider community of surviving persons with brain injury has shared with us their experiences, best advice, and insider knowledge about living successfully with brain injury and which pitfalls to avoid. Now we will share these with you.

The contents of Lesson 9 will also help you to shape doable plans to implement all of the ideas you have practiced in the preceding Lessons. Our number one recommendation will be for you to consistently use the life-long healthy coping habits described in Lessons 1 to 8. This guiding principle will be carefully detailed using two sources: (1) what providers and brain injury researchers have learned, and (2) what people with brain injury recommend. Broad, general strategies and ideas for proactive solutions to common problems will be described and demonstrated. We will help you to develop doable plans for living life successfully after brain injury.

Reviewing What You Have Learned

You have covered lots of topics as you read through your book and participated in the suggested exercises of Lessons 1 to 8. Notice the titles and content highlights of all earlier Lessons that we have put in Box 9.1. Box 9.1 contains a chart that you can use as a framework for reviewing major concepts and strategies within each of the prior eight Lessons. Try to relate your unique needs and issues to those listed as you go over each section of the chart. If your memory of the information and ideas has become fuzzy, read back through the Lessons to try to recall and grasp the content and how it is used.

You can use your book to go back over these multiple concepts and strategies you have learned through your reading and your participation in the book's exercises. Try to build a link between your own

Box 9.1 Reviewing Information, Ideas, and Strategies From Lessons 1 to 8

Lesson Number/Title	Information & Ideas	Strategies
1. Brain Injury Facts, Realities, and Inspirations	Many troubling symptoms and feelings are common and normal after brain injury Brain injury affects the family too There are many causes of injury Knowing about your injury facts and symptoms helps you feel more like yourself Knowing about rehabilitation and your provider team helps you want to work and make progress Hearing real brain injury survival stories is reassuring	Learn about common brain injury symptoms Identify your own post-injury strengths and weaknesses Get to know the different names and roles of your rehabilitation team Work as hard as you can with your rehabilitation team Read and reread this book
2. A New Sense of Self—Lost and Found	Many people with brain injury report not feeling like themselves Symptoms and recovery rates differ from person to person Symptoms are part physical, part cognitive, and part emotional and behavioral after brain injury There are many, very effective strategies for living successfully with brain injury symptoms	Identify which symptoms you have Identify how many symptoms you have of each kind Consistently use all coping strategies in this book Pat yourself on the back for your accomplishments
3. The Rehabilitation Hospital System: Staying Focused/ Positive	Rehabilitation is to improve your functioning, not cure you Rehabilitation requires your participation to work	Maintain hope Work as hard as you can Be realistic Psychologists can help with emotional adjustment

Continued

Box 9.1 Reviewing Information, Ideas, and Strategies From Lessons 1 to 8 *Continued*

Lesson Number/Title	Information & Ideas	Strategies
	Attitude and effort can affect your long-term recovery You can have mixed feelings about rehabilitation and your family members' view and role in recovery	Proactively prepare and plan for discharge home Keep communication going with family members
4. Emotional Responses to Brain Injury—Reclaiming Grief	While people with brain injury are more likely to be depressed than others, you can also be grieving normally Brain injury results in losses There are a range of normal feelings after brain injury—for the person with the brain injury and for your family members The differences between normal grief and depression What to do if you think you are depressed	Seek help from brain injury providers Recognize and accept your losses and grief If you think you are depressed, seek help and listen nondefensively to advice; follow the advice Stay positive and pat yourself on the back for even small accomplishments
5. Anger, Guilt, Acceptance, Denial, and Behavior	Anger and guilt are common after brain injury Thoughts and expectations cause these feelings Anger and guilt are destructive Thoughts are powerful Moving toward acceptance is difficult but leads to progress	Change thought patterns Change your inner negative language to more positive self-talk Adopt realistic expectations
6. Coping—How to Maintain a Healthy Outlook	There are some self-defeating thinking and attitudes that can slow progress after brain injury:	Identify whether you are thinking and looking at your situation in a self-defeating manner

Box 9.1 Reviewing Information, Ideas, and Strategies From Lessons 1 to 8 *Continued*

Lesson Number/Title	Information & Ideas	Strategies

	Self-defeating Comparisons
	   —with others
	   —you, now and before injury
	Unrealistic Expectations
	Awful-izing
	Negative self-talk
		Use the exercises and techniques in the book to avoid these thinking pitfalls
		Develop a more nurturing and positive view of yourself and your progress

7. Thoughts for People in the Life of Persons with Brain Injury	If your family member, friend, or employee has a brain injury, it will affect you You can feel shock, fear, and grief about losing the person you knew, and hopes you, had for the person All your feelings are normal Your relationship will change Nurturers can burn out There are networks of helpers for parents of children with brain injury	Ask for help from family and friends Don't let embarrassment stop you from asking for help Make your request personal Teach family and friends about the brain injury Use your state Brain Injury Association chapter—Check *www.biausa.org* See a provider with experience Compromise with other significant people in partners' lives Take care of yourself too; get respite Do what you can; don't feel guilty

Continued

Box 9.1 Reviewing Information, Ideas, and Strategies From Lessons 1 to 8 *Continued*

Lesson Number/Title	Information & Ideas	Strategies
8. Getting Support	Support groups can be helpful for recovery	Seek help with your own needs in mind
	Support groups can meet lots of needs	You can discuss most issues and concerns
	Support groups can complement the help that your friends give you	Choose a group leader with qualities that you like
	You can get feedback in support groups	Choose a group based on location, accessibility, meeting times, cost
	Support group members care about each other	Don't feel obligated to tell personal things at first
	If groups are not for you, you might want to see a peer mentor or counselor	Don't expect the group to make you better right away
	Your family might be helped by going to a support group	Ask about support groups at hospital or BI Association
		Good idea to join local Brain Injury Association; *www.biausa.org* is most reputable online site
		Be cautious about the internet and chat rooms

unique challenges and questions you have uncovered in your sessions and the information and ideas in the book. This link will increase the likelihood that you will really understand how the strategies can help you and how the book can be an ongoing resource for you. Reviewing the concepts and ideas in the order of the Lessons will be best as a structure and model for you to follow on your own.

No book about recovering from brain injury would be complete without telling persons with brain injury about the experiences of other people in the community who have been living with it, sometimes for many years. Rehabilitation providers who talk to people living with brain injury in the community report that their comments fall into two major categories: their pet peeves and their best advice for living. That is why this book will present both. We will report what community-dwelling persons with brain injury have told others about their biggest annoyances and challenges, and their best advice for living with brain injury. First, the Lesson will look at how these persons deal with day-to-day frustrations in the community. Box 9.2, "Survivors of Brain Injury Tell Us …," will present this information.

We also recommend that you read some of the books listed in the Bibliography at the end of the book, by either persons who had a brain injury and found writing about it helped them heal or by family members of persons with brain injury. You can take advantage of their learning "the hard way" by proactively reading about their challenges and mistakes rather than experiencing difficulties you are unprepared for, coping by trial and error, without their valuable insights.

Developing Your Plan to Continue the Journey of Surviving Well Day by Day

Ongoing steps toward progress and adjustment will involve developing a personal, doable plan for continuing to improve and rejoin the community in a satisfying, productive manner. You have learned your own pattern of cognitive and behavioral assets and challenges. Now the best way for you to continue to get better is to use what you have learned in combination with a proactive rather than a reactive approach. If you are proactive, you will plan ahead and think in action words. If you react, it will be after the fact and usually not as productive. Box 9.3 contains words that will lead you toward productive daily routines and accomplishments.

Box 9.2 Survivors of Brain Injury Tell Us ....

Their Pet Peeves ...	*Advice for Living Well After Brain Injury*
People tell me to be careful; tell me what to do as if they don't trust me to be safe	Count your blessings
I get tired easily	Accept your problems
I am not able to do the job I had before my injury	Know what you can and can't do
I forget what others say to me	Don't try to be someone else
I don't agree with feedback I get from others	Listen to feedback nondefensively to learn about yourself
I am not able to drive	Have doable goals for improvement
It takes me longer to do things now	Keep on using strategies you learned in rehab
People have trouble understanding my speech	Build yourself up and praise yourself for working hard
I have trouble understanding what others are saying to me	Help yourself as much as you can but ask for help if you need it
Getting generally discouraged from time to time	Know that recovery takes a long time
	Make plans and stick to them
	Exercise your body and mind
	Stay on top of stress
	Don't use alcohol or drugs
	Get involved in the Brain Injury Association

Unlike the words "avoid," or "withdraw," action words will lead to productive activity as you add them to your daily vocabulary.

In Box 9.4 we have combined the many ideas and strategies presented throughout the book with the kinds of post-injury problems they are helpful for.

Use the headings and list for proactively *planning* to address any obstacles and problems you encounter now or in your future. *Prepare* by using any of the prior questionnaires found in Lessons 1 to 8 for helping to identify post-injury problem areas. Notice that

Box 9.3 Action Words

Learn	Ask	Plan
Work	Prepare	Develop
Choose	Use	Do

the list in Box 9.4 includes the headings **_Problem, and Proactive Problem Solving._** You can **_use_** the list to first find your problem, then follow the heading to find the suggested solutions, and finally **_develop and choose_** your own unique solution. Notice that the instructions given contain several of the action words. Now we will look at an example of proactive problem solving.

Jim's Story

Jim needs to start outpatient physical therapy as he is having difficulty with balance again, even though he finished his brain injury rehabilitation three months ago. His home is too far from the physical therapy center for him to get there by foot, and it would be too expensive to take a cab back and forth. He gets confused, because of his brain injury, when he tries to tell people how to get him there and then get him back home. Using the table, under the problem "transportation," notice the solution in Box 9.4 for Jim would be to find out how to get a ride with a bus service, or a Care Van-type service.

Returning to Work or Productive Activity: Are You Ready?

People with brain injury want to be productive and many want to return to work. However, only about 39% of persons with brain injury actually return to full-time competitive employment. The reasons for this have to do with some of the cognitive and behavioral problems caused by the injury itself. Memory, extreme fatigue, impulsiveness, and concentration are among the typical problems

Box 9.4 My Go To Chart for Proactive Problem Solving

Problem	Proactive Problem Solving
Memory problems	Use schedules, to-do lists—Consistently!
	Repeat information 3 to 4 times, as often as you need to
	Write things down
	Have others remind you
	Use mnemonics like N-A-M-E
	Pay attention
Disorganized	Put all daily use or important items in one place,
	Rule: If you take it out, put it back when finished with it
	Label areas where things are stored
Always feel tired	Ask others for help when you need it
	Avoid getting too tired
	Avoid doing too much at one time
	Avoid doing frustrating tasks when tired
	Take power naps, but never after 3 p.m.
Low confidence	Talk to others for advice
	Keep a positive inner voice going
	Develop realistic goals
	Pat yourself on the back when you do even little things well
Make lots of mistakes	Avoid working on high-concentration tasks when tired
	Pace yourself in tasks rather than rush
Calculation is hard now	Use calculators
	Get help with finances from people you trust
	Work on tasks requiring calculation in quiet settings
No transportation or can't follow directions	Find out local bus or Care Van-type company schedules and ride these between destinations
	Use a Global Positioning Satellite (GPS) device in your car
	Ask a friend with GPS to drive you
Poor concentration	Turn off electronics when working on important tasks
	Do one thing at a time
	Tell yourself "Focus"
	Place your chair away from windows or doors to hallways when at work

Continued

Box 9.4 My Go To Chart for Proactive Problem Solving *Continued*

Problem	Proactive Problem Solving
Trouble communicating with others	Talk more slowly Make eye contact Talk less than your conversation partner Ask questions to clarify Don't interrupt
Few friends	Don't sit home and watch TV Get involved in community activities Volunteer to help others Use communication tips above Don't ask personal questions Ask others about themselves Don't talk too much about your injury Join national and local support organizations like Brain Injury Association
Have a hard time problem solving	Use S-O-L-V-E mnemonic Ask others for input Try to think of more than one solution Notice how people you trust and admire deal with a problem or situation like the one you are facing and copy their approach
Get angry quickly	Practice counting to 10, take deep breaths and let them out slowly, saying "relax" Ask the help of a doctor experienced in helping people with brain injury about medication for improving mood
Don't know what to tell people about my injury	It's best to make this decision based on what people need to know. You are not obligated to tell people that are not close to you
Have a hard time getting out the door in a timely manner	Hire a helper to support you during bathing, dressing, and shopping tasks until you are able to do these alone Get to bed early and keep regular hours Organize things you will need the night before

that make it challenging for persons with brain injury to look for, find, and keep a job. You should ask yourself some very important questions before attempting to return to work.

1. Am I ready to work?

2. Can I afford to work?

3. Do I receive disability income that might be reduced if I work?

All of these questions must receive careful thought prior to looking for a job. For example, with regard to item 1, patients must be able to get to the location of work by driving or by public transportation. Endurance is another readiness consideration. What are your normal waking and sleeping hours? What time of day do you feel sleepy and for how long? With regard to item 2, being able to afford going to work, you may need to think about expenses due to daycare for children, uniforms, transportation, and equipment. Finally, related to item 3, disability income affects the choice of whether to work because you may jeopardize your income by working too many hours.

There are various points along the journey back to work after brain injury, each with its own set of considerations and challenges. There is a time for just getting ready to go out there and look, which involves considering any potential obstacles to working and how to overcome these if they exist. Then, there is a time of actually seeking a position. Finally, once hired or once a volunteer position has started, there are special issues related to keeping that position. There are also community-based agencies, clubhouses, or day programs that are specifically focused on vocational services and supports for persons with brain injury. Ask one of your rehabilitation providers for contact information such as web addresses, information and telephone numbers, and locations of these potential resources.

Returning to Work: Obstacles and Aids to Preparing to Work

When you begin to consider returning to work or starting to do volunteer work, you should try to do as much as possible to remove potential obstacles and take advantage of proactive aids to realizing your goals. Potential *obstacles* include sleeping late and staying up too late, not having set habits and routines, difficulty with fatigue, cognitive deficits, costs of work, and lack of confidence. Look back and reread Lessons related to improving endurance, compensatory cognitive strategies, and proactive problem solving for guidance in overcoming those obstacles. Aiming for regular bed times, improved sleep hygiene, better nutrition, and better self-pacing will help you overcome these obstacles. It will also be important to avoid negative self-talk and to work toward setting realistic goals. Look through your book to find the prior Lessons that address these issues. Possible costs of working include daycare, uniforms, and transportation. The potential *aids to overcoming the obstacles* include setting doable goals, getting organized, consistent and purposeful use of compensatory cognitive strategies, and use of a work mentor. With regard to the work mentor, you should look for someone who you trust, who is working, and who will give you encouraging feedback and information without asking to be paid.

Returning to Work: Actual Job Search and Application

Making a good impression through first contacts, interviews, and résumés that are focused but impressive to potential employers can be challenging after brain injury. Fortunately, there are some excellent ways to improve the likelihood that you can make the best impression possible, despite difficulties with speech, memory, concentration, and nervousness. For example, knowing what your strengths and weaknesses are will be critical for making sure you make a good match between your abilities, preferences, and any position you accept or seek. Look back at one or more of the many questionnaires related to your specific post-injury challenges that you have taken during the reading of this book. Make a list of your strengths and your weaker areas. Following these two lists, complete the "Vocational Decision-Making Process Form" in Box 9.5 whenever you are considering a job or volunteer opportunity. Notice that after your strengths and weaknesses, you are asked to put something about the kind of work you like. If you have considered doing any particular work lately, use the form to detail whether the job would be a good match for you. If you are not able to name a recent job search, try to complete the form using the exercise in Box 9.5.

Joe's Story

Joe was a stock clerk in a drug store. Stock clerks often have late afternoon or evening hours, work inside, have to record small numbers from bottles and products onto a sheet, keep track of items on aisles, and replace them when they get low, etc. Using the form in Box 9.5, list the duties of a stock clerk under the heading "My Potential Job Facts." Now write down what work you like to do and your strengths and weaknesses. When you finish filling in that row, compare the items with your work preferences and strengths, and decide if the job of stock clerk would be a good match for you.

Look back at Lesson 2, where active listening techniques and best social behavior for making friends are described. If you recall, when you use active listening techniques by not dominating the conversation or interrupting, you can improve your communication with others. Improved communication and behavior can improve all social relationships, not just work-related relationships.

You might want to use a work mentor. A mentor is someone who can be trusted, usually a working person, who can advise you without asking for money. Good mentors will be encouraging and helpful but will not do your work for you. Many people with brain injury report that using a work mentor helps when writing applications and résumés, deciding on which job to apply for, and trying to deal with stress on the job.

In writing a résumé, choose a style that presents qualifications and abilities rather than leading with dates worked. In this way, any gaps in your work history will not stand out so much. Examples of these alternate formats are featured in Boxes 9.6 and 9.7.

Try these formats out. Write in your work skills or prior jobs held in the format, and notice the dates you worked become somewhat less prominent and the qualifications are highlighted. Use of these different formats will help minimize work history gaps that may have

Box 9.5 Vocational Decision-Making Process Form

My Strengths	My Weaknesses	Work I like To Do	My Potential Job Facts
		Examples: outdoors, indoors, at a desk, alone, use of my hands, use of computer	

occurred following the brain injury. The alternate formats will also help present your abilities and qualifications in the best possible light.

For the interview itself, use advice for social communication provided in Lesson 2 when you practice for and participate in job interviews. Interviews are, after all, a kind of social situation. Our best advice for making a good impression during an interview is to be on time, make good eye contact, dress neatly, avoid falling asleep, avoid

Box 9.6 Sample Résumé Format To Maximize Work Skills

Skill	Jobs Held (with dates)
Skill	Jobs Held (with dates)
Skill	Jobs Held (with dates)
Qualifications:	

Box 9.7 Sample Résumé Format To Maximize Jobs Held

Job Held	Date:
Job Held	Date:
Job Held	Date:
Qualifications:	

making inappropriate comments, and wait before answering to make sure that you have fully understood the question. Interviews are nerve wracking for most people. People who try to give good answers and ask good questions as well as project a positive outlook will be able to manage this nervousness once they are actually in the interview. Look back at Lessons that address stress management techniques for additional help with pre-interview jitters.

Returning to Work: Enhancing Job Stability

Once you have a job or start volunteering, there will be issues that arise that may lead to worry about keeping a job because of having a brain injury. There are stressful situations and difficult people to deal with at any job. There are demands that could lead to fatigue and a feeling of being overwhelmed. Those two statements are true for anyone, and a brain injury increases the chances that they will threaten job stability.

Several Lessons of your book can be applied to the work-setting and the day-to-day coping that is required for staying in a job. In particular, Lessons 2, 4, and 5 dealing with mood, coping, self-management of feelings, and problem solving hold important ideas for insuring job stability. The review chart in this Lesson (Box 9.4) lists relaxation techniques, positive self-talk, and taking care of oneself as strategies that make it more likely that a person with a brain injury can deal effectively with day-to-day stressors at work.

Several other approaches will improve your chances of keeping a job. For example, when starting a job, you should take your time to get to know the people and system as each setting has its own way of doing things. In that way you will not run the risk of being seen as pushy and overbearing. In addition, maintaining the same good grooming, outlook, self-care, and plan for avoiding mistakes will be as important for your job stability as it was for the interview phase. Mistakes and social blunders, falling asleep on the job, and taking a haphazard approach to assigned tasks can also be avoided through careful, proactive, and consistent use of compensatory strategies covered in several of the Lessons. Look back through all your Lessons for more ideas for coping.

Summary

Lesson 9 is full of guidance and ideas. The charts for reviewing preceding Lessons, for discovering what tips survivors of brain injury can give you about challenges and living successfully, about "Action Words," and about "Proactive Problem Solving," as well as the "Vocational Decision-Making Process Form," and the purpose and potential uses for each, can help you plan and deal with many situations. You are to be congratulated for your work and what you have learned by reading this book and engaging in its exercises. You now are armed for the life-long journey of living with brain injury. You have both general wisdom about brain injury and an understanding of your own unique injury and recovery story.

Bibliography

American Psychiatric Association. (2000). *Diagnostic and Statistical Manual* (4th ed.), pp. 349–356, Washington DC: American Psychiatric Association.

Bauser, N. (2001). *Acceptance Groups for Survivors*. Bloomington, IN: 1st Books Library.

Brain Injury Association of America. (2007). *The Essential Brain Injury Guide* (4th ed.). McLean, VA: Author.

Brain Injury Association of Minnesota. (2009). *Peer Mentor Support Connection Program Policies*. Unpublished document.

Condeluci, A. (1995). *Interdependence: The Route to Community* (2nd ed.). Winter Park, FL: GR Press.

Crimmons, C. (2000). *Where Is the Mango Princess? A Journey Back from Brain Injury*. New York: Random House.

Ellis, A., & Harper, R.A. (1977). *A New Guide to Rational Living*. North Hollywood, CA: Wilshire Book Company.

Gonzales, P. (2007*). Support Group Facilitator Guide*. Minneapolis, MN: Brain Injury Association of Minnesota.

Gottman, J., Notarius, C., Gonso, J., & Markman, H. (1976). *A Couple's Guide to Communication*. Champaign, IL: Research Press.

Niemeier, J. P., & Kreutzer, J. S. (2001). *First Steps Toward Recovery from Brain Injury*. Richmond, VA: National Resource Center for Traumatic Brain Injury.

Niemeier, J. P., Kreutzer, J. S., and DeGrace, S. M. (2009). *Choosing, Finding, and Keeping a Job After Brain Injury*. Wake Forest, NC: Lash Associates.

Olkin, R. (1999). *What Psychotherapists Should Know About Disability*. New York: Guilford Press.

Osborn, C. L. (2000). *Over My Head: A Doctor's Own Story of Head Injury from the Inside Looking Out*. Kansas City, MO: Andrews McMeel.

Swanson, K. L. (2003). *I'll Carry the Fork! Recovering a Life After Brain Injury*. Scotts Valley, CA: Rising Star Press.

Taylor, J. B. (2006). *Stroke of Insight*. New York: Viking.

West, D., & Niemeier, J. P. (2005). *Memory Matters: Strategies for Managing Everyday Memory Problems*. Richmond, VA: National Resource Center for Traumatic Brain Injury.

Williams, M. B., & Poijula, S. (2002). *The PTSD Workbook*. Oakland, CA: New Harbinger.

Woodruff, L. (2008). *In an Instant: A Family's Journey of Love and Healing*. New York: Random House.

Glossary

Acceptance. Typically, emotional and cognitive state in which there is little or no distress regarding current status, but after brain injury is best thought of as an emotional and cognitive state in which any distress present minimally interferes with current functioning and satisfaction.

Acquired brain injury. Includes brain injury due to traumatic brain injury (both open and closed head injuries), stroke (both occlusions and hemorrhagic), tumors, infection, and anoxic/hypoxic, but typically not including congenital conditions or progressive conditions, though in some settings may be used more inclusively.

Americans with Disabilities Act (ADA); Americans with Disabilities Act Amendments (ADAA). Two federal laws designed to protect the rights of persons with disabilities.

Aneurysm. An outgrowth or weakness in a brain blood vessel or artery that can burst and cause bleeding in the brain (hemorrhagic stroke).

Anger. An emotion typically entailing distress about the actions of other people.

Anosognosia. See *Denial, organic*.

Anoxic brain injury. See *Hypoxic brain injury*.

Behavior management. Techniques used to help persons with brain injury be safe, while maximizing the benefit from acute rehabilitation or community-based care.

Brain, function. Cognitive processing (e.g., concentration, memory, learning, reasoning). Also entails emotional and behavioral processing.

Brain, organic. Brain structure or physiology.

Brain injury. Changes in brain function, structures, or physiology.

Brain Injury Association of America. A non-profit organization whose mission is "Creating a better future through brain injury prevention, research, education and advocacy." Has multiple state chapters (e.g., Brain Injury Association of Minnesota, Brain Injury Association of Virginia).

Closed head injury (CHI). A type of traumatic brain injury in which there is no skull fracture. Sometimes imprecisely used to include all brain injuries, even those not involving trauma.

Cognitive. Information processing (e.g., concentration, memory, learning, reasoning), as opposed to feeling processing (emotions) or actions (behavior).

Cognitive Behavioral Therapy. Several strategies that are used to help people compensate or cope with many everyday problems, not just injury related problems.

Cues. Verbal, visual, or physical (e.g., at tap on the shoulder) reminders to help a person know when to do something or when to use a strategy.

Denial, organic. Inability to see problems because the brain supplies inaccurate/incomplete information due to brain injury.

Denial, psychological. Avoidance of problems because something is too painful to admit as being true, even though known to be true by the person.

Guilt. An emotion typically entailing distress at one's own actions.

Hypoxic brain injury. An injury to the brain caused by low oxygen. Sometimes confused with **anoxic brain injury**, which is a more severe type of injury caused by total lack of oxygen.

Independence. Being able to function without help, but since no one actually is totally independent, it is best thought of as having sufficient relationships that one can achieve goals with less interference from limitations because of support.

Interdependent. A state in which one exists in a web of relationships that are mutually respectful and focuses on abilities, with recognition that functional limitations are often due to system failures. See writing of Dr. Condeluci.

Interdisciplinary therapy. Speech therapy, physical therapy, occupational therapy, recreational therapy, music and art therapy, psychology, social work, nursing, etc., with awareness that services between disciplines overlap.

Medications. Several kinds of prescription drugs that are used to help reduce problems related to the brain injury.

Multidisciplinary therapy. Services provided by a team of therapists. See *Interdisciplinary therapy*

Open head injury (OHI). A type of traumatic brain injury in which there is a skull fracture.

Physiatrist. A physician who specializes in rehabilitation.

Psychologist, neuropsychologist. A psychologist who specializes in organic changes to the brain. Typically conducts neuropsychological evaluations of changes in brain function, but in some rehabilitation settings may also conduct counseling.

Psychologist, rehabilitation. A psychologist who specializes in response to injury or disability and integrates cognitive, emotional, behavioral, social, and societal factors. Typically provides counseling for response to disability (and counseling for families), but in some rehabilitation settings may also conduct cognitive evaluations of brain function.

Stroke. An injury to the brain caused by (1) a buildup of fat deposits on arterial walls that eventually block blood flow, or (2) a clot that forms and travels in the arteries and obstructs blood flow (embolism or embolic stroke), or (3) bleeding in the brain. See *Aneurysm*.

Subarachnoid hemorrhage. Bleeding under the arachnoid covering of the brain.

Subdural hemorrhage. Bleeding under the dura or outer covering of the brain.

Supported employment. Services provided by agencies that help people get back to work after brain injury. Often they provide staff who accompany persons with the brain injury to work for support and help in adjusting to the work setting.

Traumatic brain injury (TBI). An injury to the brain caused by (1) direct blunt force to the head (like with an object, or when the head hits the dash in a car accident), (2) the brain moving rapidly back and forth such as in a car crash, but which may not require the head actually striking anything, or (3) a penetrating object like a bullet. Sometimes imprecisely used to include all brain injuries, even those not involving trauma.

Tumor, brain. A mass that is growing in any part of the brain and causing cognitive and functional impairments because of pressure or destruction of brain cells. The tumor may be removed surgically and, in the process, some healthy tissue around the tumor may be affected.

About the Authors

Janet P. Niemeier, PhD, ABPP, is an Associate Professor of Physical Medicine and Rehabilitation and Director of Inpatient Neuropsychology and Rehabilitation Psychology at Virginia Commonwealth University Health System (VCUHS) in Richmond, Virginia. She has 25 years of experience in assessment, treatment, advocacy, teaching, and research about persons with brain injury and other disabilities. She has worked to improve quality of life and effectiveness of interventions for this client population in private practice, outpatient treatment facilities, and in inpatient hospital settings.

Dr. Niemeier has a strong record of externally funded research with a primary focus on establishing effectiveness of treatments for persons with brain injury. She currently has support from the National Institutes of Health (NIH), the National Institute of Disability Rehabilitation and Research (NIDRR), and the Virginia Commonwealth Neurotrauma Initiative Board (CNI) to do trials of her methods. Dr. Niemeier has developed comprehensive as well as skill-specific interventions, including the Lighthouse Strategy for improving visual neglect following stroke or traumatic brain injury and a manualized intervention for helping clients get back to work after brain injury. Findings of her trials of these methods are published in first tier scientific journals, giving clinicians the confidence that they are using evidence-based methods in their efforts to enhance cognitive and functional skills for their clients. Dr. Niemeier serves on grant application review committees for NIH as well as the Department of Veteran's Affairs, advising committee members about the challenges and needs of persons with brain injury. She is active as a speaker in the Virginia Brain Injury Association and has served as their support group facilitator.

Dr. Niemeier is author of the books, *First Steps Toward Recovery From Brain Injury, Memory Matters,* and *Choosing, Finding and*

Keeping a Job after Brain Injury. She has authored dozens of articles in scientific journals, and has been invited speaker for hundreds of national and international conferences, seminars, lectures, papers, and workshops. She is faculty sponsor for the VCUHS physician residents' Journal Club.

Dr. Niemeier is a Fellow, and current President-Elect, of Division 22, Rehabilitation Psychology, of the American Psychological Association. She is also Board Certified by the American Board of Professional Psychology as a Rehabilitation Psychologist and serves as Secretary of the Board. As Secretary she oversees the National Board certification process of Rehabilitation Psychologists.

Robert L. Karol, PhD, ABPP, is president of Karol Neuropsychological Services & Consulting, a group private practice in Minneapolis, MN, specializing in the evaluation and care of persons with acquired brain injury. He was the Director of Psychology/Neuropsychology at Bethesda Hospital in St. Paul, MN for twelve years and was Director of Brain Injury Services.

Dr. Karol co-founded the Brain Injury Association of Minnesota, serving on its Board of Directors for fourteen years and he is a past Chairman of the Board. He has advised the Minnesota Department of Human Services regarding brain injury on its Traumatic Brain Injury Program Advisory Committee, its Neuropsychological Services Ad-Hoc Committee, and its Needs of Adults with Brain Impairment Committee. His work includes having been on the Board of Directors of Accessible Space, Inc., a provider of brain injury residential programming, and on the Advisory Committee of TBI Metro Services, a provider of brain injury vocational services. He served on the Minnesota Department of Corrections Traumatic Brain Injury Expert Advisory Panel. Organizations including hospitals, residential care providers, prison correctional institutions, and insurance companies have utilized his consultation services. He has also taught as an Adjunct Professor at Argosy University.

He is the author of the book *Neuropsychosocial Intervention: The Practical Treatment of Severe Behavioral Dyscontrol After Acquired Brain Injury* and a book chapter about brain injury care: *Principles of behavioral analysis and modification.* His most recent article is *Neurobehavioral Crisis Hospitalization: On the Need to Provide*

Specialized Hospital Brain Injury Crisis Programming. He has given more than 135 workshops, seminars, lectures, and papers.

Dr. Karol is Board Certified by the American Board of Professional Psychology as a Rehabilitation Psychologist and is Certified by the Academy of Certified Brain Injury Specialists (ACBIS) as a Certified Brain Injury Specialist Trainer (CBIST).

Index

Note: Page references followed by '*f*' and '*b*' denote figures and boxes, respectively.